ic Literature
Developing Environmental Awareness
Through Children's Literature

ALSO BY NANCY LEE CECIL

WITH PATRICIA L. ROBERTS AND SHARON ALEXANDER

*Gender Positive! A Teachers' and
Librarians' Guide to Nonstereotyped
Children's Literature*
(McFarland, 1993)

WITH PATRICIA L. ROBERTS

*Developing Multicultural Awareness
Through Children's Literature*
(McFarland, 1993)

*Developing Resiliency
Through Children's Literature*
(McFarland, 1992)

Developing Environmental Awareness Through Children's Literature

A Guide for Teachers and Librarians, K–8

by NANCY LEE CECIL

McFarland & Company, Inc., Publishers
Jefferson, North Carolina, and London

Cover art by Diane Perruzzi.

British Library Cataloguing-in-Publication data are available

Library of Congress Cataloguing-in-Publication Data

Cecil, Nancy Lee.
　　Developing environmental awareness through children's literature :
a guide for teachers and librarians, K–8 / by Nancy Lee Cecil.
　　　p.　cm.
　　Includes index.
　　ISBN 0-7864-0221-0 (sewn softcover : 50# alk. paper) ∞
　　1. Environmental sciences — Study and teaching (Elementary) — United
States — Bibliography.　2. Environmental sciences — Study and teaching
(Secondary) — United States — Bibliography.　3. Environmental
sciences — Study and teaching (Elementary) — United States — Activity
programs — Bibliography.　4. Environmental sciences — Study and
teaching (Secondary) — United States — Activity programs —
Bibliography.　I. Title.
Z5863.P6C43　1996
[GE105]
016.3637 — dc20　　　　　　　　　　　　　　　　　　　　　96-2361
　　　　　　　　　　　　　　　　　　　　　　　　　　　　　　CIP

©1996 Nancy Lee Cecil. All rights reserved

*No part of this book, specifically including the table of contents and index,
may be reproduced or transmitted in any form or by any means, electronic or
mechanical, including photocopying or recording, or by any information
storage and retrieval system, without permission in writing from the publisher.*

Manufactured in the United States of America

*McFarland & Company, Inc., Publishers
　Box 611, Jefferson, North Carolina 28640*

To Jane Ducey, with love

Contents

Preface   1
  Readings   3
Introduction   5

Literature for Grades K–3   7
  Realistic Contemporary Fiction   9
  Folk Literature   41
  Fanciful Fiction   55
  Historical Fiction   57
  Biographies   61
  Information   64

Literature for Grades 4–8   99
  Realistic Contemporary Fiction   101
  Folk Literature   120
  Fanciful Fiction   126
  Historical Fiction   130
  Biographies   134
  Information   143

Index   171

Preface

Environmental awareness can be actively fostered by strong teacher-models who demonstrate their own conviction that becoming environmentally aware is something that *all* Americans, young and old, can do together, and that this view is worthwhile and achievable. Such teachers can also foster environmental awareness while increasing literacy skills by introducing children to literature that has at its core main characters who are themselves in the process of becoming environmentally aware.

Follow-up discussions of the literature can show children that there is more than one solution to environmental problems such as those related to natural resources protection, tree planting for future forests, and development of environmental technology, and that they, like the literary characters, can contribute to the solution of these problems. Moreover, retelling the same stories through dramatic play or other activities can place children into the roles of problem-solvers and allow them, for a while, to be transformed into fictional characters who embody problem-solving behavior that they will need to live in a changing environment.

One example from literature that could be selected is Aliki Brandenburg's *A Weed Is a Flower* (Simon and Schuster, 1968). This biography features George Washington Carver, a strong African American man, who learns to survive physically and emotionally by relying on himself. The book reveals what he learns about the importance of his environment, and how he creates wonderful products from one of nature's plants. By relying on his skills as an agriculturalist chemist, Carver convinces farmers to grow peanuts as a crop. In his laboratory, he makes approximately 300 products from peanuts, such as animal food, soil fertilizer, soap and ink.

A follow-up discussion to this book would underscore the range of alternatives open to Carver — some positive and others negative. An environmentally unaware child would likely see Carver's situation as "just something that happened because Carver was a chemist," whereas the same circumstance would probably be viewed more optimistically by the more environmentally aware child, who could more easily relate to Carver's inventiveness in looking

Preface

at the environment and studying what he saw. The teacher's role, then, would be to guide the less-aware children into seeing the situation from a more environmentally-aware point of view. The teacher would help the children brainstorm some possible paths Carver could have taken when he found himself in a seemingly hopeless situation. The teacher could then ask the children to speculate about the effect of such actions.

The teacher could also show children how Carver became a "hero of the environment." The teacher could point out that Carver worked his way through school and graduated from Iowa State College of Agriculture. He joined the staff at Tuskegee Normal and Industrial Institute in Alabama and contributed his life savings to the George Washington Carver Foundation for Agricultural Research, a museum of his discoveries. Today, the George Washington Carver National Monument is on the farm where he was born and is a symbol of his environmentally positive legacy. Finally, having those same children role play a strong character like Carver would allow them to "try on" Carver's behavior, and perhaps over time, grow in their own understanding of how scientists can create new products from plants found in the environment.

Using children's literature to foster awareness of a topic is not new. Bibliotherapy, the use of books to help children understand the problems of life, is a practice dating back to the time of Aristotle, when the architects of the libraries of ancient Greece inscribed such inscriptions as "the medicine Chest for the Soul." There is little doubt that by empathizing with believable book characters, children may be able to understand better the environmental problems faced by others. When children read about a character who is environmentally aware, as Carver was, they can reach into themselves to make adjustments or react to changes in a myriad of actions that might also have been taken. And with children's literature, as opposed to real life situations, no one sits in judgment of the readers' decisions.

A teacher who believes in protecting the environment — and who also models the idea that we can and must do so at once — can encourage children to develop related awareness behavior. Additionally, carefully chosen children's literature, which has as its center those stories associated with environmental awareness, can provide fictional dilemmas that allow children to exercise the problem-solving skills necessary for facing future frustrating and difficult environmental situations in real life. With a guided discussion about a range of alternative solutions, children can begin to see that they have the capacity to contribute to the solution of some of the environmental problems in their own lives. Also, by donning the role of fictitious citizens in children's literature through dramatic play, children further increase their repertoire of problem-solving skills.

Preface

In the following sections, teachers will find some helpful books that will allow them to use children's literature as a vehicle for fostering environmental awareness. The first two sections contain short summaries of carefully selected children's books, each of which features main characters who are environmentally aware. These characters have faced environmental problems. These book summaries each identify particular environmental foci that are highlighted and also indicate the grade level(s) for which the book would be most appropriate.

The book summaries are divided into two subsections. First are books suitable for young children; these are the picture story books, which are generally used with primary students. Some, however, contain more sophisticated concepts and can be used with older children, as noted. Second are the books suitable for older students; these are the multi-chaptered, nonpicture books that are generally targeted to intermediate grade children and often provide a more in-depth study of the character and ordeal. The two sections are then further subdivided by literary genre, and each subsection includes examples of realistic contemporary fiction, folk literature, historical fiction, biography, fanciful fiction and informational books.

Target activities are provided for each book to help children internalize the concepts in the text and focus on environmental awareness.

Developing Environmental Awareness is intended only to be a starting point for teachers who find themselves concerned by the fact that their students will soon face major problems related to the environment, and to a larger and larger degree, who may be in need of problem-solving skills that will help them rise to these challenges. While even the most committed educators cannot by themselves change the environment of the children in their charge, they can become positive role models as adults who maintain a concerned stance about protecting the environment. Furthermore, teachers can enhance their language curriculum by placing quality children's literature into carefully planned activities that will guide the children toward developing the problem-solving skills necessary for thriving in today's changing times. This book is a writer-to-reader "literary step" toward that end.

Readings

Appleberry, M. H. (1989). "A Study of the Effect of Bibliotherapy on Third Grade Children Using a Master List of Titles from Children's Literature." University of Houston. University microfilm 69–21, 746.

Beardsley, D. A. (1979). "The Effects of Using Fiction in Bibliotherapy to Alter Attitudes of Regular Third Grade Students Toward Their Handicapped Peers." Unpublished Ph.D. diss., The University of Missouri–Columbia. University microfilm 80–07, 128.

Preface

Bissett, D. J. (1969). "The Usefulness of Children's Books in the Reading Program." Paper presented at the International Reading Association, April 30–May 3, Kansas City, Missouri.

Bodart, J. (1980). "Bibliotherapy: The Right Book for the Right Person at the Right Time — and More." *Top of the News* (36), 183–88.

Brocki, A, C, (1969). "New Literature for Inner-City Students." *English Journal* (58), 1151–61

Cianciolo, P. J. (1985). "Children's Literature Can Affect Coping Behavior." *Personnel and Guidance Journal* (43), 897–903.

Cornett, C. E. and Cornett, C. R. (1980). "Bibliotherapy: The Right Book at the Right Time." *Fastback 151.* Bloomington, Ind.: Phi Delta Kappa Educational Foundation. ED 192 380.

Koon, J. F. (1970). "Cues for Teaching the Emotionally Disturbed: Turn On, Tune In, Drop Out. *The Clearing House* (44), 497–500.

Nigen, G. A. (1979). "Bibliotherapy for the Atypical Reader." *Wisconsin State Reading Journal* (24), 12–16.

Schultheis, M., and Pavlik, R. (1977). *Classroom Teachers' Manual for Bibliotherapy.* Fort Wayne, Ind.: Benet Learning Center. ED 163 493.

Squire, J. R. (1968). Response to Literature. Champaign, Ill.: National Council of Teachers of English.

Zaccaria, J. S. and Moses, H. A. (1988). Facilitating Human Development Through Reading: The Use of Bibliotherapy in Teaching and Counseling. Champaign, Ill.: Stipes.

Introduction

In recent years, many Westerners have become increasingly aware of the part the natural environment plays in determining the quality of their lives. Perhaps no single goal will be more important in our future efforts to pursue the public happiness and quality of life than that of improving our environment. This goal, I believe, is one that will help define a new spirit for the twenty-first century, a new expression of our idealism, and a new challenge that will sorely test our ingenuity. This goal can be met, but only if we give it the same priority that Theodore Roosevelt did when he described dealing with conservation and proper use of natural resources as "the fundamental problem which underlies almost every other problem of our national life."

There are noble reasons for protecting the environment — one might argue that it is our moral duty, as good citizens of the planet, not to destroy its natural wonders. There are also pragmatic reasons — the vanishing rainforests contain pharmaceuticals we might need to survive; the Antarctic holds a vast store of fresh drinking water; thick forests ensure that we will have oxygen to breathe. But the best reason is older and less tangible, a matter of ecopsychology: we need a healthy, thriving, bustling natural world so that we can feel whole. It is no coincidence that our word "whole" comes from the same ancient root as "holy." It was, apparently, one of the first concepts that human beings needed to express, and it meant the healthy interrelatedness of all things. Perhaps that is why we call our planet "Mother Earth."

If we are to significantly improve our environment in the months and years ahead, then all of our people must join in a united effort to do so. Strong environmental action will be necessary, at all levels. But, additionally, private citizens and voluntary groups must join in the crusade. So must businesses and industries, labor and farm organizations, scientific and especially educational institutions — every part of our society. It is important, too, that the quality of our environment continues to be seen not as a national, but as a global concern of all people young and old.

Now that the world has seen the planet as it appears from outer space, all people of all nations can appreciate it more clearly than ever before as their

Introduction

common home — small and round and one — with a thin and precious atmosphere on which we all depend, and with no artificial boundaries to divide our energies or keep us apart. Humankind has applied a great deal of energy in the past to exploring this planet. Now we must make a similar commitment of effort to restoring that planet. Our scientific capacity has grown to such a degree that we may someday be able to reside in places other than earth; yet our glimpse of its beauty from outer space has only reminded us of how very much we cherish earth's qualities. Reversing environmental deterioration will be one of the major goals of the next generation, involving all the main functions of society. It will not be enough to cope with each environmental atrocity as it reaches the point of imminent danger to life and health.

This book sets forth the proposition that the children of the United States — the future leaders of tomorrow — must be instilled with an uncompromising love, respect, and understanding of our environment. If this transformation can occur, then our current environmental ills will no longer pose a serious threat to Western civilization.

Literature for Grades K–3

Realistic Contemporary Fiction

To foster environmental awareness needed by today's world inhabitants, it is essential that we learn to care realistically for our environment within our technology. While fiction can never substitute for hands-on contact with the environment, carefully selected children's books can develop ecological awareness and deepen understanding of environmental problems and the various solutions that are needed. Rather than being the apocryphal ostriches-in-the-sand who are unable to see what's going on in their habitat, children need to discover what is important in their environment and what is needed to maintain it.

An important topic of study and action in today's classrooms is awareness of the impact we make on the environment — ecology. Supporting this study, a wide range of well-informed, balanced, and well-presented children's literature is available that portrays our effect on the environment and the value of caring for it conscientiously.

As you search for books pertinent to caring for the environment, you'll be pleased to find that environment-caring authors and artists have included young children in preschool and the primary grades (K–3) as an audience for their writings and drawings. For example, Bonnie Pryor's *The House on Maple Street* (Morrow, 1987, 1–3) gives an honest study of changes in the environment over three hundred years and may cause youngsters to think about changes that have happened in their area over time. The house on Maple Street stands on land where a forest once grew and wild animals lived. A forest fire started by lightning burns the area, then grasses grow back and buffalo come to eat the grass. Native Americans hunt the buffalo for their food and clothing. One clan spends the summer there and a father shows his son how to form an arrowhead — which the boy loses. The Native Americans move away and wagon trains stop by the stream for water. A couple remains there and builds a log cabin. Finally, present-day children are seen playing in the yard behind the house.

Grades K–3

Among other fine examples, several are especially suitable for kindergarten and the primary classrooms. *In the Small, Small Pond* (Holt, 1993, K) by Denise Fleming is stunning in its exploration of animals and their activities around a small pond as the seasons change. *The Alphabet in Nature* (Children's Press, 1991) by Judy Feldman is an enjoyable way to look at nature as it explores the shapes of letters of the alphabet that are found in photographs of animals and nature scenes. It also provides relevant information about nature and its creatures to the beginning nature lover when it shows such scenes as a close-up of the fangs of a black-and-green African bush viper, a Monarch caterpillar changing to a chrysalis, and grass magnified under a microscope.

Several hundred new children's books are published each year in addition to videos and films, tapes, and other products about the environment and ecology. These annual offerings, added to older titles and the audiovisual materials still in print, make up a wide range of possibilities for selecting environmental material for children. Since no child can interact with them all, this section is available to help you select appropriate titles for children. The contemporary realistic selections discussed in the following section include a variety of settings, plots and characters.

1 Albert, Richard E. (1994). *Alejandro's Gift*. New York: Chronicle.
   Environmental Focus: Appreciating the wilderness of the Southwest
   Living a solitary life in the desert, old Alejandro enjoys the wild animals that are attracted to the water he uses to irrigate his garden. When the animals visit, he doesn't feel so alone, so he decides to install an artificial water hole near his home to benefit his desert friends. Unfortunately, none of them visit. He knows the creatures are thirsty so he must figure out *why* they won't come. The book provides an insightful look at wilderness and how humans can observe its wonders with more than just their eyes. The glossary includes illustrations and brief descriptions of plants and animals that inhabit the Southwestern United States. K–3.
   Target Activity: "Predictive Web"
   When reading this delightful book aloud to children, stop at the point where the animals do not come to visit the man's artificial water hole. Ask children to brainstorm some reasons why the animals will not come. Have older children write a brief paragraph (younger children may pictorialize their answer) telling what they think the man should do to attract the animals to the water. Finally, finish reading the story and have children compare what they thought the man might do with what he actually did.

Realistic Contemporary Fiction

2 Allen, Judy (1993). *Whale.* Illustrated by Tudor Humphries. New York: Greenwillow.
Environmental Focus: Conserving Earth's animals

Anya and her family are returning home from a nearby island when they hear on their boat's radio about a terrible oil slick. As she is thinking about this, Anya spies something in the water and is amazed to find it is a humpback whale and her little calf. They are in trouble and may be drowning. Just as her mother convinces Anya there is nothing they can do to help the whales, the rest of the herd comes by to rescue their herd members. Anya notices that some of these whales have gashes in their sides where they have been harpooned and are injured themselves, but still they persist in helping the mother whale and her calf. The whales are saved and go safely back out to sea. The book contains special endnotes about what is currently being done to save the whales. 2–3.

Target Activity: "Describe the Whales, Save the Whales"

During a discussion of the importance of saving whales, secure a recording of whale sounds and show the children pictures of whales. Invite children to brainstorm their ideas about what these animals might be saying to one another. Ask the children to describe different whales and guide them into a describing sequence from simple to complex.

To do this, begin by asking children what they see and encourage them to call the object by name and color. Next, engage children in describing all of the features of the object and the details in the setting. If desired, turn this into a game activity and challenge the children to respond in one of four ways when an illustration is shown. Give descriptive directions as children volunteer for their group, i.e., "Please describe it by name" or "Please describe it by name and color" or "Please describe it by name and color and features" and "Please describe it by name and color and features and setting." If desired, points can be given to the groups as descriptions are given. Encourage children to use their descriptions of whales when they write for information about whales.

For more information about the plight of the whales and what children can do to help them, have them write letters to the following address:

Save the Whales
P. O. Box 3650
Washington, DC 20007

3 Aschenbrenner, Gerald (1988). *Jack, the Seal and the Sea.* English adaptation by Joanne Fink. NJ: Silver Burdett.
Environmental Focus: Caring for Earth's natural resources

Grades K–3

In this story containing a warning to humankind, a young man named Jack spends his days sailing on the sea and pulling in nets that contain half-dead fish. The ocean is polluted but Jack doesn't seem to care, until one day he finds an ailing seal and receives an urgent message from the ocean about its sordid condition. Jack gives up his life as a fisherman so that he can spread the message of the ocean to the rest of the people. K–4.

Target Activity: "Recycle, Reduce, and Reuse"

Every person is responsible for the plight of our environment, including our oceans — even the person who increases the amount of garbage that accumulates by the end of each day. Read the poem "Sarah Cynthia Sylvia Stout" by Shel Silverstein from *Where the Sidewalk Ends* (Harper and Row, 1974). Have children write down five ways Sarah could decrease the amount of garbage she uses by applying the three R's that will save our environment: Recycle, Reduce, and Reuse. Ask children to sketch ways that they recycle, reduce, and reuse materials to take care of their environment and display their drawings on a classroom mural.

4 Baylor, Byrd (1976). *Hawk, I'm Your Brother*. Illustrated by Peter Parnall. New York: Charles Scribner's Sons.

Environmental Focus: Observing nature's creatures

In the Santos Mountains, Rudy Soto wants to fly like a hawk. He spends hours watching them before he steals a baby redtail hawk from its nest. Seeing the hawk caged and resentful, Rudy releases the bird and watches it fly away. He feels he is flying together with the bird in spirit. They call to one another as one brother would call to another. Seeing the wild hawks fly makes Rudy Soto yearn for the birds' sense of autonomy exemplified through their ability to fly. To Rudy, flying is a symbol of a sense of control over life. 2–3.

Target Activity: "I'm Your Brother"

Give the children an example of something in the environment that you imagine you can be "a brother to" (for example, a tree) and tell them why. Then reread the excerpt where Rudy releases the bird and feels he is flying with the bird in spirit. Invite individuals to tell something they can be "brothers" or "sisters" to and encourage them to give reasons for their responses.

Additionally, discuss with children that in this book, and in another Baylor book, *The Desert Is Theirs* (Charles Scribner's Sons, 1975), there is a relationship between humans and earth shown through the Papago Indian culture that emphasizes sharing with the earth and not taking from it. With children, discuss the theme; it points out what humans can learn from the animals and plants that adapt to the sun and the scarce water supply in the desert. How does the theme of learning from nature relate to the earlier Baylor story?

5 Berkey, Helen (1967). *Aunty Pinau's Banyan Tree.* Illustrated by Raymond Lanterman. Rutland, VT: Charles E. Tuttle Co.
Environmental Focus: Recognizing the value of trees

A common sight in Hawaii is the giant banyan tree, its huge mass supported by roots growing down from the branches to the ground below. This engaging story of one such banyan tree — Aunt Pinau's banyan — begins when the Little Wind gets a clothesline full of clean laundry all dirty. Aunty Pinau tries to buy a "wind catcher" and, to her young nephew Jo-Jo's surprise, comes back with a tiny banyan tree.

Through the years, with Jo-Jo's loyal care, the tree grows strong, putting out more and more roots until finally, the tree can provide lots of relief from the hot Hawaiian sun. Mynah birds live in the tree and women string their leis in it shade. Mr. Matsumoto serves shaved ice to schoolchildren and the fishermen find shade under its branches. One day, however, the town mayor decides that a highway should be constructed and that its course will mean chopping down the beloved banyan tree. Aunty Pinau decides it is time to send the surveyors packing and to teach the mayor a thing or two. The tree is saved. 2–3.

Target Activity: "A City Official in the Classroom"

Invite a city or county official to class to talk to the children about the reasons why they preserve trees or remove trees when constructing new county or city buildings. Ask the official to give real examples of ways trees have been protected in the environment. After the visit, engage children in writing thank-you letters to the official and telling what they learned. Additionally, children can contact the following group for further information on how they can protect a tree and the animals that live in it:

The Wilderness Society
900 17th Street, NW
Washington, DC 20006

6 Birchall, Brian (1974). *Kahee the Cautious Kiwi.* Illustrated by Hadley Hodgkinson. Auckland, NZ: Golden Press.
Environmental Focus: Recognizing the kiwi as a protected bird

Grades K–3

In this colorful text, we follow Kahee the kiwi's life from his initial home in the roots of a great rimu tree to his life as the companion of a young boy who extricates him from a trap that has caught the animal's leg. When the boy's teacher explains to him that kiwis are protected birds, the class arranges to take him back to the bush after his leg has healed. Kahee is returned to "his own kind" back in his own bush where he is happiest. K–3.

Target Activity: "Protected Birds and Animals"

Help children find out about birds and animals that are currently on the protected list in the area in which they live. Discuss why they are protected and what the children can do to keep the animals from becoming extinct. For older children who wish to, have them retell the story of Kahee, The Cautious Kiwi, substituting a new protected bird or animal about which they have studied, e. g., "Sammy, the Sad Spotted Owl" or "Lily, the Timid Leatherback Turtle." Invite them to illustrate their stories and create a classroom book entitled "Protected Birds and Animals."

7 Brown, Margaret Wise (1954). *Wheel on the Chimney*. Illustrated by Tibor Gargely. New York: J. B. Lippincott.

Environmental Focus: Appreciating nature's creatures

This story portrays the natural cycle of life of the storks in Europe, where many people believe that it is good luck to have a stork nest on the roof. To attract the storks, some homeowners tie wheels to their chimneys, hoping the birds will settle there. In spring, two storks build a nest in the wheel on a chimney and the reader follows the birds' migratory stages as they fly south to Africa in the winter and return to Northern Europe the following spring when instinct guides them back to their nests. 1–2.

Target Activity: "Understanding What Books Say About Storks"

With a small group, show the picture book *Wheel on the Chimney*, or another favorite book about storks, along with a picture dictionary. Ask children to share any myths that they have heard concerning storks. Guide the children in telling how the two books are alike and how they are different on the subject of storks. Identify each of the two books and ask someone to select a page in each book. Read the pages, or parts of each page, to the children. Guide them in explaining how they would use each book if they wanted to know more about storks and how the birds live in the environment. If desired, repeat the activity with another type of reference book.

Realistic Contemporary Fiction

8 Brown, Mary Barrett (1992). *Wings Along the Waterway.* New York: Orchard.
Environmental Focus: Learning about wetland birds
Exquisite full-page drawings of 21 wetland birds are accompanied by text that explains the birds' appearance, behavior, and habitats. The book lacks a range map, but its absence might motivate advanced students to research and make one. 3 & up.
Target Activity: "We're All Wet"
For the duration of this study, each child might " adopt" a wetland animal and research its behavior, habits, and habitat. The child might make a three-dimensional model, costume, or drawing, and then write a monologue or skit, create a chart, prepare a protest speech about the animal's endangered status, or undertake another project to tell about the animal. The children's presentations could be made to classmates, other classes, or to the parents on a "We're All Wet Celebration Day."

9 Bunting, Eve (1993). *Someday a Tree.* Illustrated by Ronald Himler. New York: Clarion.
Environmental Focus: Observing trees
Under a large oak tree on the family's land, a family hold their picnics, take naps, tell stories. However, one day young Alice sees that the grass under the tree "smells funny" and is yellow. When its leaves start to fall, the tree is visited by a tree doctor who finds out that the soil has been poisoned by illegally dumped chemicals. Everyone in the neighborhood joins together to carry away the poisoned dirt. Firefighters spray clean water around the tree and some people wrap sacking around its top branches. Employees of the local telephone company donate poles for sunscreens to shade the tree. When the tree dies in spite of the care, Alice recalls her collection of acorns and plants them in the ground near the dead tree. K–3.
Target Activity: "Noticing What Is Going On in Nature"
Invite the children to role-play Alice and be observant about nature as they take a nature walk near the school in the neighborhood. Ask them to look for the unusual signs of something going wrong in nature and sketch what they see:
1. grass that is turning yellow;
2. leaves falling from trees;
3. plant life that "smells funny."

Invite them to complete their sketches when they return to the classroom and to tell more about what they noticed on the walk. If leaves of trees are

Grades K–3

collected, introduce *A B Cedar: An Alphabet of Trees* (Orchard Books, 1989) by George Ella Lyon or a similar source. *A B Cedar* is an alphabet of trees that identifies leaves and expresses ways trees help us with "Air and food / Shade and wood / Trees give us a stair to climb / a place to look / even this book!" Additionally, *Canadian Trees A–Z* (Grasshopper Books, 1989) by Colleayn O. Mastin is a rhythmic, lighthearted way for children to be introduced to Canada's trees. The verses have factual information, are suitable to read aloud, and are easily learned by young children, i.e., "The maple leaf on Canada's flag; Is well-known even in Europe; / This tree gives us excellent furniture wood, / As well as some great maple syrup."

10 Butterworth, Nick (1992). *One Blowy Night.* Illustrated by the author. Boston: Little, Brown.
Environmental Focus: Understanding the feelings of animals

One night, Percy the park ranger needs to help his animals find a new home after a fierce storm knocks down the giant oak tree in which they had lived. The book is enhanced and balanced by Butterworth's illustrations that poignantly convey the animals' feelings of loss and hope as Percy listens and responds to their plight. At the end of the story, a foldout poster that reveals the animals' new home will elicit surprise and discussion from young readers. K–3.

Target Activity: "Natural Disasters and the Impact on Animals"

Butterworth's book is unique in that it portrays a natural disaster from the perspective of "lesser" living creatures; we generally consider only the impact on humans.

Ask children to select a natural disaster — a flood, tornado, earthquake, forest fire, blizzard, etc. Then ask them to select a wildlife creature. Encourage them to write a short story about the disaster through the eyes of the animal — perhaps writing about the heroic rescue of the animal after the disaster. Remind them that animals are unusually vulnerable, but that human beings may intervene to help out, just as Percy did, and just as humans may choose to help out in real life. Lead a general discussion about how children can consider their own pets when their family is making emergency preparedness plans.

11 Cameron, Ann (1988). *The Most Beautiful Place in the World.* Illustrated by Thomas B. Allen. New York: Knopf.
Environmental Focus: Appreciating spectacular beauty in nature

Abandoned by his parents, seven-year-old Juan lives with his grand-

Realistic Contemporary Fiction

mother in the mountains of Guatemala. It is a place of spectacular beauty where volcanoes rise from the shores of the blue lake and brilliantly plumed wild parrots flock in the trees. Juan must work to support his grandmother by shining shoes in front of the Tourist Office. Although he is a positive thinker and is grateful for his life and his grandmother, he secretly dreams of better things. And more than anything, he would like to go to school. His wish is granted. 2–3.

Target Activity: "The Most Beautiful Place in the World"

Juan's grandmother tells him, "The most beautiful place in the world is anyplace you can be proud of who you are." Juan adds, "and when you love somebody a whole lot and you know that person loves you — that's the most beautiful place in the world" (p. 57). Ask children to discuss both the grandmother's and Juan's point of view. Do they agree or disagree? Why or why not? Invite children to share the place they feel is the most beautiful place in the world. Ask them if the beauty is because of their feelings about the place, or if they think everyone would agree that the place is beautiful. Discuss the expression "beauty is in the eye of the beholder." Guide children to see the meaning of this expression as it applies to the story.

12 Carlstrom, Nancy White (1990). *Blow Me a Kiss, Miss Lilly.* Illustrated by Amy Schwartz. New York: Harper & Row.

Environmental Focus: Appreciating the way a garden can fulfill a purpose in a child's life

Sara, a young girl, responds to the death of her elderly friend, Miss Lilly. Miss Lilly lives with her cat Snug across the street, and Sara is often there helping in the garden or the kitchen, and talking to her friend. Each time Sara leaves, they both throw kisses as their way of telling each other they are friends. When Miss Lilly becomes ill, Sara sends a get-well card with the message, "Blow me a kiss, Miss Lilly." Sara's sadness over her friend's death is eased somewhat by taking care of Snug and seeing the flowers blooming in the spring garden. K–2.

Target Activity: "Messages a Garden Sends"

Select and display books about gardens and, when possible, select pages relevant to children's interest to read aloud. Focus discussion on the messages that are sent by planting and caring for a garden. Other titles to consider on this subject are Anita Lobel's *Alison's Zinnia* (Greenwillow, 1990) in which girls with names from A to Z present flowers to one another and send the message of friendship; *Alphabet Garden* (Macmillan, 1993) by Laura Jane Coats, which is an alphabetical tour of a child's actions and observations in a backyard

Grades K–3

garden, and *Growing Vegetable Soup, Planting a Rainbow,* and *Eating the Alphabet* (all Harcourt Brace Jovanovich, 1987, 1988, and 1989 respectively) by Lois Ehlert, which are all stunning in their bright watercolor presentations of fruits, vegetables, and flowers.

Further, invite children to try to explain Sara's real message when she wrote, "Blow me a kiss, Miss Lilly," on the get-well card. What was Sara trying to say? Encourage children to design get-well cards for anyone they know who is ill and to dictate or write their messages for friends, relatives, or family members.

13 Caudill, Rebecca (1964). *Pocketful of Cricket.* Illustrated by Evaline Ness. New York: Holt, Rinehart & Winston.

Environmental Focus: Appreciating one of nature's insects

On an August afternoon, six-year-old Jay carries a cricket home in a wire-screen cage. The cricket lives in his bedroom until September, when Jay takes the cricket to school in his pocket because he is reluctant to leave it behind at home. Jay's understanding teacher asks him to show his chirping pet to the class. Intimate relationship of child and pet develops and is supported by Jay's relationship with his understanding teacher. The teacher shows sympathy for the small boy's need for something familiar (and friendly) near him on the first day of school. K–2.

Target Activity: "Jay's Cricket"

Jay did not want to be far away from his pet cricket. So, Jay decided to "write" with a mix of pictures and words (a rebus record) and tell about some of the happenings with his pet — things like the cricket living in a wire-screen cage, his surroundings in the bedroom, his journey to school in Jay's pocket, and his debut as a chirping cricket in the classroom. Have children draw some of the pictures for a rebus record that Jay might have drawn. Have them share their pictures with others.

Further, show the children pictures of crickets and secure a recording of nature sounds including the sounds of crickets. Ask the children to describe the pictures of the crickets and present facts about the cricket, where it lives, how and when it makes a chirping sound, and so on. Play the cricket sounds on the recording and invite the children to tell when (what season?) and where (generally in rural areas) they have heard this sound.

Realistic Contemporary Fiction

14 Clark, Ann Nolan (1941). *In My Mother's House.* Illustrated by Velino Herrera. New York: Viking.

Environmental Focus: Appreciating the love of nature of a young Pueblo Indian boy

Though out-of-print, the book is worthwhile to find in the branch libraries because it shows the experiences of a young boy's life as a Pueblo Indian: "I string them together / Like beads. / They make a chain, / A strong chain, / To hold me close / To home, / Where I live in my Mother's house." Illustrations and text have details from the world of Pueblos about the Council, Fire, Home, Mountains, Pasture, People, and Wild Plants. A young Pueblo Indian boy lets readers inside his heart and mind as he puts his thoughts about his mother and his home into words. 1–3.

Target Activity: "Recognizing a Strong Link to the Environment"

With children, discuss the things in the Indian boy's life that link him closely to his environment — mountains, pasture, wild plants — and also discuss the things in the children's lives that link them to their own environment. Invite the children to draw their own interpretation of their environment. Ask the children to write one feeling they have about their environment beside their drawings. Each feeling is to describe something in their lives that ties them to their environment. Display the environmental drawings in the classroom.

15 Davis, Deborah (1989). *The Secret of the Seal.* Illustrated by Judy Labrasca. New York: Crown.

Environmental Focus: Recognizing the bond between humans and animals

Using initiative and resourcefulness, Kyo, a young Eskimo boy, protects his playmate — a seal pup — from his uncle, the hunter. Young Kyo goes out to kill his first seal and discovers a bond between himself and the female seal that he names Tooky — originally his quarry. Kyo tries to prevent the capture of his new animal friend which triggers a clash between traditional and modern values and a conflict in loyalties. 2–3.

Target Activity: "A Bond Between Kyo and the Seal Pup"

Encourage children to discuss the ways Kyo established a relationship with his seal pup playmate. How will the children try to explain the conflict between his uncle's traditional values toward hunting and Kyo's modern values about caring for the seal pup? Ask children if they can imagine any time when it would be appropriate to kill animals. Invite children to relate their own experiences about caring for nature's animals to the story.

Grades K–3

Optional Activity: "Feelings about Hurting Animals"
Ask each child in the class to think about his or her personal feelings about hurting animals. What experiences have made them feel the way they do? The children may or may not choose to share their feelings in the discussion. Finally, ask each child to dictate / write a brief paragraph or draw a picture summarizing his or her personal feelings about hunting. If possible, invite a hunter or trapper who earns his livelihood from this pursuit into the classroom to offer another point of view about this topic.

16 Ehlert, Lois (1991). *Red Leaf, Yellow Leaf.* New York: Harcourt.

Environmental Focus: Fostering an appreciation for trees
A sugar maple tree taken from the forest, tended in a nursery, purchased, and finally planted by a young child grows and matures with the seasons. Brilliant collage illustrations and an informational afterword make this book very useful across the primary grades. K–2.

Target Activity: "A Tree Fair"
Take children on a walk around the area to pay special attention to trees. Inspired by the beautiful illustrations, children can be encouraged to create their own collages of their favorite trees in their yard or neighborhood. Using the information in the encyclopedia or in the afterword of the book, help children to discover the name of their favorite tree. Transcribe the name of the tree on the bottom of each child's collage. Finally, have a tree fair and have students display their collages, encourage them to share the information they have learned about the importance of trees, and gather together other books on trees for browsing.

17 Ets, Marie Hall (1965). *Just Me.* Illustrated by the author. New York: Viking.

Environmental Focus: Enjoying creative imaginings related to nature and nature's creatures
Playing on a farm and in the woods, a young boy mimics the characteristics of different animals he sees. He prowls like a cat, struts like a rooster, hops like a rabbit, and slithers like a snake. After playing in the cornfield, he tries to get his father's attention and runs to catch up with him. Joining his father by the pond, the boy climbs into the boat at the water's edge and they motor out together.

Target Activity: "Seeing Different Images of Fish in a Pond"

To foster an appreciation for the beauty of goldfish, introduce the children to the poem "Calling Me" in *Balloons and Other Poems* (Farrar, Straus & Giroux, 1990) by Deborah Chandra. Chandra offers children a different image of the shape, texture, sound / lack of sound and movement of goldfish in a pond who open wide their mouths as if "they're calling...calling me." Chandra writes, "I watch them call, / Their lips grown round; / It's strange — / I never hear a sound." Give the children an example of something different that you imagine about a goldfish in a pond and tell them why. Invite individuals to tell something that they imagine about a goldfish and encourage them to give reasons for their responses.

18 Ets, Marie Hall (1955). *Play with Me*. Illustrated by the author. New York: Viking.

Environmental Focus: Appreciating nature

Going into a meadow to find some animal companions and to play, a small girl frightens some of the living creatures who want to come close to her. She scares away a grasshopper, frog, turtle, chipmunk, bluejay, rabbit and snake. Unhappy about this, the girl sits down on a rock by a pond and quietly and intently observes the actions of a waterbug. While she is sitting so still and quiet, the creatures return and her composure is rewarded by a fawn who licks her on the cheek. Pre–1.

Target Activity: "Embellish a Story with Poems about Nature"

With the children, reread the story, stopping at a place where a creature is introduced and inserting a few lines of poetry about the creature. Useful for the embellishment are several poems from *One at a Time* (Little, Brown, 1980) by David McCord, recipient of the National Council of Teachers of English award for contributing to excellence in poetry for children.

19 Fradin, Dennis B. (1978). *Bad Luck Tony*. Illustrated by Joanne Scribner. Englewood Cliffs, NJ: Prentice-Hall.

Environmental Focus: Caring for one of nature's animals

Tony is looking forward to a visit by his eccentric grandfather who lives in a mobile home and doesn't like to stay in one place for too long. He is eager to develop a relationship with his grandfather, although he has not seen him since he was a baby. At the same time, Tony finds a stray pregnant dog and is trying to find a warm, safe place in which the animal can have her puppies. He goes all over town looking for a home for the dog with no luck. Finally, Tony convinces his grandfather that he should stay with him and his mother until Christmas and wait for the dog to have her puppies. Christmas morning, the dog has her puppies in the driver's seat of the grandfather's mobile home. The grandfather decides to take the dog and puppies with him on his next journey. He also agrees to visit Tony more frequently in the future. Tony is clearly not a quitter, and his strong determination leads to a positive solution concerning the dog, and to a burgeoning relationship with his grandfather. 2–3.

Target Activity: "Finding a Home for a Puppy"

Invite a representative from the local SPCA to speak to the class. Discuss with her what could be done to find homes for the stray animals. Divide the students into three groups to explore the following three topics:

1. What information should people have about the responsibility of owning a dog before acquiring a puppy?

2. How could people who would like a dog find out about animals that might be available at the SPCA?

3. What could you do if you found a stray animal roaming the streets?

20 Frank, Phil (1994). *The Greenpatch Gang in the Case of the Contaminated Canine.* New York: Harcourt Brace.

Environmental Focus: Solving problems about pollution

When his dog becomes ill, Bodie and his friends trace the problem to poisoned water in a storm drain. Their investigation to determine the source of the pollution leads them to uncover a case of illegal dumping of industrial waste. The story's comic book format will appeal to newly-independent readers. The pictures are black and white and there is much information at the back of the book about storm drain pollution and how children can get involved in solving such problems in their own neighborhood. A portion of the book's proceeds will be donated to the protection and restoration of native forests. K–4.

Target Activity: "Letters to the Editor"

Bring in a local newspaper and read children some of the editorials that concern local pollution and illegal dumping problems, or problems that concern the local water supply. Explain that what Bodie and his friends did, though dangerous, was one way to effect change in a community. Another way is to write letters to local officials asking them to investigate the problems and try to do something about them. Have each member of the class select the local problem that most concerns him or her and help each write a letter to the appropriate local official. For younger children, provide an expository frame with the structure of the letter already completed. As replies come in, share them with the entire class.

Realistic Contemporary Fiction

21 Freeman, Don (1974). *The Seal and the Slick.* Illustrated by the author. New York: Viking.

Environmental Focus: Caring for Earth's animal resources

A seal pup is caught in the detritus of an oil slick spilled during an offshore oil rig accident. Covered with oil, the young seal barely makes it to shore where he is aided by two very caring young people. They scrub him with a special cleaning agent and, fortunately, are then able to turn him loose to return to his family. K–3.

Target Activity: "Caught in the Debris"

What is it like for animals to become entangled in debris made by humans when the animals are unable to free themselves, as the seal in the story found himself? A simple hand exercise will demonstrate the feeling to children in the class. Have children take rubber bands and loop the bands around their thumbs, stretch them over their hands (not the palms) and then loop them around their little fingers. Ask the children to pretend that their hand is a seal entangled in some litter. Without using their other hand or any other parts of their bodies, urge them to try to free themselves from the rubber bands. As they soon discover, it is almost impossible to remove the rubber band. They are vicariously experiencing the helpless feeling that many entangled animals experience. Afterwards, ask children how they think the animals feel. What advice would they give to people who are careless about our environment?

22 Jam, Teddy (1993). *The Year of Fire.* Illustrated by Ian Wallace. New York: McElderry.

Environmental Focus: Understanding the effects of fire on the environment

In a Canadian maple grove where a grandfather and his granddaughter are sugaring, he tells her about a fall forest fire years ago that blazed through a village in the grove. The effects of the fire were covered by falling snow but, unknown to the people, the fire was smoldering all winter in the tree roots of the remaining maple trees. When spring came, the snow melted and all the trees fell over. Its unusual ending takes the story out of conventional reflection about the past. K–3.

Target Activity: "Fighting a Fire to Save the Environment"

Review some of the details of the story by asking the children to relate them to their experience and ask, "what has happened to someone you know that is similar to the time in this story?":

1. when the father realizes that his children had joined him to fight the fire?
2. when one of the children is singed by the fire and loses his eyebrows?

3. when the mother throws empty pails out the door so the others can fill them with water?

4. when the fire burns down the school house and lessons have to be taught in the church?

5. when the people were surprised because the trees all fell over in the springtime?

Optional Activity: "Smokey the Bear Says"

Design and make "Smokey the Bear" coloring books for the young learners in the school. Have a local forester or wildlife expert check it for accuracy before it is distributed. Show the children how fires can be both positive and negative. Also show them that only trained foresters can set fires for forest management; the rest of us — when camping, hiking, gathering wood, and so forth, need to remember what Smokey the Bear continues to say, "Only YOU can prevent forest fires!"

23 King, Patricia (1958). *Mabel the Whale*. Illustrated by Katherine Evans. Chicago: Follett Publishing Co.

Environmental Focus: Caring for wildlife

In this Beginning-to-Read book, Mabel the whale is captured from her home in the Pacific Ocean by a group of men in a ship. Mabel is put in a tank in Marineland so that people can come and watch her swim by looking through the glass sides of the tank. The tank is too small, however, and the hot sun burns Mabel's fin; she becomes very sick. Mabel is moved by a huge crane to a bigger tank. A veterinarian gives Mabel some shots and Mabel is happy again, making everyone in Marineland happy. K–2.

Target Activity: "A Home for Mabel the Whale"

Review with children the events of Mabel's transfer from the Pacific Ocean to a tank and then to a larger tank. Where do they think Mabel was the happiest? Why? Also ask children to consider why Mabel was brought to the aquarium. Did the people who captured her have a good reason for doing so? Help children to write a letter, as if they were Mabel, either to the men on the ship that captured her, or to the caretakers at Marineland, telling them how she feels about leaving the blue waters of the Pacific Ocean.

24 Krudop, Walter Lyon (1993). *Blue Claws*. Illustrated by the author. New York: Atheneum.

Environmental Focus: Appreciating life on the beach

Visiting his crusty, rough grandpa who lives alone in a shack on the beach, a small boy describes his first search for "Blue Claws," a type of crab inhabiting the beach environment. The grandfather-grandson relationship is a tenuous one at first when the two go fishing and the boy is rebuked for not knowing how to fasten the boat to the dock correctly. However, as the catch of crabs increases, the relationship grows friendlier and the two enjoy watching the sights of nature. K–3.

Target Activity: "Animal Adaptation"

Assign students to find a picture or make a drawing of a kind of marine or other animal that has a special adaptation — for example, pincers on crabs, long necks on giraffes for reaching high leaves, and so forth.

Conduct a class discussion on the value of different kinds of adaptation of sea creatures and other animals. As a part of the discussion, share with children the idea of the thumb as an adaptation in humans.

Pool all of the students' pictures or drawings of adaptations and categorize them through the use of the writing board or overhead into the following categories:

- body shape (puffin fish)
- coloration (emphasize camouflage of the young, e.g., the fawn)
- mouth type (emphasize creature's feeding behavior, e.g., the turtle)
- reproduction (turtles)
- other categories that the children establish

25 Lasky, Kathryn (1993). *My Island Grandmother.* Illustrated by Amy Schwartz. New York: Morrow.

Environmental Focus: Appreciating nature's seasons

Returning each year to an island off the northeastern coast, Amy and her parents and her grandmother spend their summer enjoyably. Amy goes with her kind, patient grandmother to explore the island — explorations which make Amy remember her grandmother long after the family has returned home at the end of summer and her grandmother has gone back to her city life. K–2.

Target Activity: "Exploring Nature Through Anecdotes"

After reading the story aloud to the children, review the good times that Amy and her energetic grandmother enjoyed on the island by inviting the children to relate what Amy and her grandmother did to their own experience. What anecdotes with family members or friends can the children tell about picking berries, watching ducklings hatch, or swimming in natural and safe ocean-side pools? How would their lives be different if there were no more natural environments left? On what occasions have the children told stories with others about cloud shapes, sky constellations, and sailing on the sea?

Grades K–3

Transcribe children's stories about exploring nature and allow children to illustrate them and put them into a class book.

26 Lyon, George Ella (1990). *Come a Tide.* Illustrated by Stephen Gammell. New York: Orchard Book/Watts.
Environmental Focus: Coping with nature's flood waters
In March, in the hills, it rained and snowed for four days and nights. Grandma said, "It'll come a tide," and it did. Four families cope with the flood, gather family members, find a boat, and ride to higher ground. The rains wash away chickens, gardens, pigs, and porches. When the flood stops, they return to "make friends with a shovel." This family persists in spite of the flooding waters, copes with the trouble it causes — getting to higher ground — and all survive the potentially dangerous situation by working together to clean up the mess left by the flood. PreK–2.
Target Activity: "Surviving in the Environment"
With children, talk about the characters in the story — Grandma's prediction, family and neighbor cooperation, and the escape from danger by working together. Discuss the meaning of "Making friends with a shovel."
By looking through as many newspapers as they can, students cut out all articles they find that remind them of the characters, events, or idea of cooperation in *Come a Tide*. Articles may include reports on rescues, stories of survival during natural disasters, and stories of cooperation for a bulletin board display or a class album. Have students link experiences in the book to experiences in real life by dictating or writing one or two sentences linking the news article to a similar character or event from the book and placing the sentences next to the article on a page in the album or on the display.

27 McCloskey, Robert (1957). *Time of Wonder.* Illustrated by the author. New York: Viking.
Environmental Focus: Enjoying living near the ocean
This story portrays the daily activities of a family during some summer weeks as they vacation on an island off the coast of Maine. They go boating, swimming and exploring. They see the changes in the land, water, plants, animals, and weather that ranges from fog to sunshine. At the end of their vacation, a hurricane blows in, sending a signal of summer's end. 1–3.
Target Activity: "Releasing a Creature of the Ocean"
Discuss that in a Western state, members of several animal rights groups,

"In Defense of Animals," "Action for Animals," and "People for the Ethical Treatment of Animals (PETA)" have advertised a plea for people to press for the release of Shamu, a killer whale that has been in captivity at Sea World for 23 years, and to boycott theme parks. By contrast, a veterinarian has pointed out that the whale would never survive in the wild, for she looks to humans for her food now. The risk of releasing her is too great and she would not survive in the wild. Ask the children to prepare for a round table discussion of this problem after role-playing such roles as a) the director of a whale research station who says that Shamu's pod (group of whales that travel together) still roams the Pacific ocean between Alaska and Vancouver and that the whale should be released; b) a member of an animal rights group that says the whale should be released; and c) a veterinarian who thinks releasing the whale is a fanciful activity and that the other whales will not know who she is nor accept her; and a biologist who says he can introduce the whale into her original pod slowly and help her adjust to having to capture her own food.

28 Major, Beverly (1993). *Over Back.* Illustrated by Thomas B. Allen. New York: HarperCollins.

Environmental Focus: Appreciating nature and finding a special place

Wearing her jeans and T-shirt, a determined young African American girl goes "over back" and finds a safe and special place of her own. She interacts with nature as she rides a cow, discovers a salamander, and finds some frog eggs. 1–3.

Target Activity: "Motions for a Nature Outing"

With children, review the illustrations and write their dictated sentences about each illustration on the board or on an overhead transparency. Return to the dictated list and ask children to pretend they are going "over back" too, and they may suggest motions to accompany the dictated sentences about interacting with nature. Have children suggest movements for running "over across the fields, back behind the barn" as well as for the following, and then ask them to act out the motions for each:

- turning over a rock and discovering a salamander;
- looking into the creek and finding frog eggs;
- taking off your shoes and wading barefoot in a creek;
- picking blueberries from a bush;
- tasting and eating handfuls and handfuls of blueberries;
- seeing the flower of the pink arbutus and sneaking close and smelling its fragrance;

- trying to get on the back of a cow and then having your first ride on a cow through the pasture and the fields back behind the barn; and
- returning home.

29 Martin, Charles E. (1985). *Island Rescue.* Illustrated by author. New York: Greenwillow.

Environmental Focus: Surviving in the wilderness

The story is told of life on an island when an emergency occurs. After the island children have a spring picnic, Mae wanders off to pick wildflowers. Jonathan finds her and realizes she is injured. He alerts the other children who quickly go for help while Jonathan and another child stay to comfort Mae. The adults call the Coast Guard and Mae's mother, who come at once. One of the Coast Guard members makes a splint of soft branches and some napkins for Mae's broken leg. Mae is carried to the truck on a stretcher and there taken by Coast Guard boat to the hospital on the mainland. A few days later, Mae returns to a cheering crowd. K–2.

Target Activity: "Surviving in the Wilderness"

Ask children to recall sequentially the chain of events that allowed Mae's injury to be swiftly taken care of in the hospital. How did the children use common sense? What could Mae have done or not done to avoid the accident? Find information about the Coast Guard and share with children how they help keep people safe on bodies of water all over the country.

Optional Activity: "Safety in the Wilderness"

On the chalkboard or overhead list two columns, one headed "safe" and the other "unsafe." After reading *Island Rescue* with children, ask them to brainstorm what actions occurred that were "unsafe" in the wilderness environment (e.g., wandering off alone) and what actions were "safe" (e.g., deciding that one child should stay with Mae while another goes for help). Have children make wilderness safety posters out of construction paper, using mottos derived from the safe list, such as "Always hike with a buddy" or "Don't wander off the trail!"

30 Mayer, Anne (1991). *The Salamander Room.* Illustrated by Steve Johnson. New York: Knopf.

Environmental Focus: Caring for one of nature's creatures

Brian finds a salamander in the woods and wants to keep it for a pet. Instead of just saying no, his mother asks him a series of questions designed

Realistic Contemporary Fiction

to make Brian consider the habitat needs of the creature: Will he miss his friends? Where will he sleep? What will he eat? Where will he play? As the young boy tries to make the salamander's new home as much like its natural habitat as possible, he begins to see why wild creatures are much better off in the woods. The illustrations are wonderfully detailed creations that show the reader the woods that are the salamander's home; Johnson has captured the soft colors of the woods with sunlight filtering through. K–3.

Target Activity: "The Right Habitat for an Animal"

Ask children for a show of hands of those who have pets. Using a bar graph, chart which animals the children in the class have. Using the most popular pet in the class, draw a Venn diagram on the writing board or overhead and place the popular pet over one circle and "salamander" over the other.

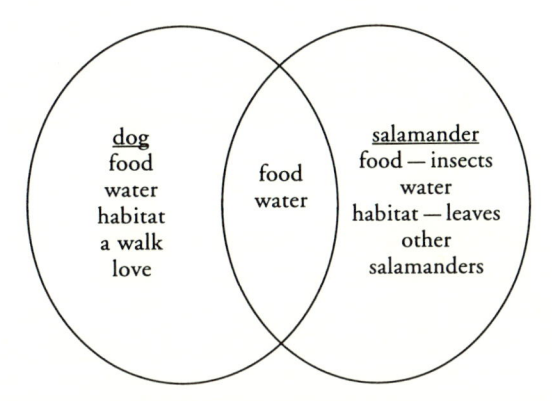

<u>dog</u>
food
water
habitat
a walk
love

food
water

<u>salamander</u>
food — insects
water
habitat — leaves
other salamanders

Have children name all the environmental needs of the domestic pet and then place those in the one circle. Have them list the environmental needs of the salamander and place them in the other circle. Place common needs in the circle overlap. Ask children if they can now articulate why wild animals are not popular pets.

31 Miles, Miska (1971). *Annie and the Old One*. Illustrated by Peter Parnall. Boston: Little, Brown.

Environmental Focus: Recognizing the natural evolution of seasons, time and people's destiny.

Annie lives on the Navajo Indian Reservation with her grandmother, called the "Old One," her father, her mother, and a herd of sheep. She helps tend the sheep and garden and goes to school. She lives a happy life until she learns from her grandmother that when the new rug being woven by her mother is completed, her grandmother will go back to Mother Earth. Since her grandmother means so much to her, Annie feels she must do something to prevent this from happening. She attempts to keep her mother from weaving the rug by misbehaving at school and by letting the sheep out of the corral at night to distract her mother. Both these ploys fail, as the teacher is merely amused by Annie's antics, and the sheep do not wander far. Annie then resorts to stealthily unweaving the rug at night and is caught in the act by the Old One. The Old One then takes Annie aside, out into the mesa, and points out the natural evolution of seasons, time, and destiny. With this, Annie realizes that "she was a part of the earth and the things on it. She would always be a part of the earth, just as her grandmother had always been, just as her grandmother would always be, always and forever." Annie gains a deep, unspoken realization of the inevitability of earth's natural order, and accepts this way of life. The next morning, Annie starts weaving the rug. 3.

Target Activity: "Annie Learns about Natural Evolution"

Discuss what students have learned about Annie. Annie is very close to her grandmother and relies on her to explain life and to help her understand who she is. She cannot imagine living without the "Old One." Annie is fearful of the time when the new rug is finished, for her grandmother has said, "My children, when the new rug is taken from the loom, I will go to Mother Earth." Annie finds it difficult to accept her grandmother's aging and death. Write descriptive traits on the board. Brainstorm some ideas about how Annie will be feeling when the rug is finished; several years later, when Annie is grown up and has children; or when Annie is an "Old One." Determine what values Annie has learned from the Old One and how she would carry them into later life. Ask children to choose one of Annie's later stages and write several sentences about what her life is like at that time.

32 Peters, Lisa Westberg (1990). *Good Morning, River!* Illustrated by Deborah Kogan Ray. New York: Arcade.

Environmental Focus: Listening to a river "talk"

Through the seasons, Katherine has a special relationship with Carl, her elderly neighbor, and she looks forward to hearing him yell at the river in a booming voice each morning; it seems that the river always answers him softly. When Carl's illness forces him to move away, all is quiet at the river. When he returns, and is able to talk only in whispers, Katherine is the one to make the river talk again as the special relationship continues to grow. Katherine learns about the river and its resounding water from Carl; he is the only one

Realistic Contemporary Fiction

who can make the river resound until he loses his voice and then Katherine yells to the river in her own loudest voice, "Good Morning!" K–3.

Target Activity: "What's in a River?"

Discuss Carl's love of the river. Ask children to brainstorm some of the positive aspects of a river, e.g.,

- We can swim and fish in the waters of a river;
- Rivers provide water — for drinking, for farming, for recreation;
- Rivers are used for transportation; and
- Fish and plants live in rivers.

If possible, take a field trip to the river nearest your school. Have children record in notebooks all the various plants and animals that they see (these can be written or pictorial, depending on the grade level). Have them also observe the ways they see the river being used by humans.

Back in the classroom, provide trade books or simple research material about specific fish or other animals that live in this river. Ask groups of children to discover three new facts about these fish or animals to present to the rest of the class.

For older children who are interested in keeping their river free of pollution, suggest that they contact the following organization:

Trout Unlimited
800 Follin Lane SE, Suite 250
Vienna, VA 22180-4959

33 Sheldon, Dyan (1991). *The Whales' Song.* Illustrated by Gary Blythe. New York: Dial.

Environmental Focus: Fostering an appreciation for whales

Lilly's grandmother tells her the story of what the whales meant to her when she was a child, how she used to bring them special gifts, and how her friends often thought that whales were "magic." Lilly constantly dreams of whales and brings them a pink flower as a present. One night she goes down to the shore and sees the whales jumping, leaping, and singing. Maybe she is dreaming; maybe she is not, but Lilly is sure she hears the whales calling her name. The oil paintings that accompany this memorable text are absolutely breathtaking. The book is a "must" for helping children develop empathy for and interest in whales. K–3.

Target Activity: "Song of the Whales"

Obtain a tape of whale communication or "singing" that is available commercially or through a nature store. Have children close their eyes and try to imagine these large animals jumping, leaping, and singing, as Lilly did. Ask children why they think Lilly's grandmother thought whales were "magic"? Invite children to share what it is that they think the whales are saying to one another or singing to one another.

Finally, borrow a tape or CD of *Don Quixote* by Gordon Lightfoot and play the song "Ode to Big Blue" about a sperm whale in the ocean. The libretto contains many interesting facts about whales that add to the children's appreciation of these majestic creatures.

34 Simmons, Dawn Langley (1993). *The Great White Owl of Sissinghurst.* Illustrated by S.D. Schindler. New York: McElderry.
   Environmental focus: Fostering an appreciation for owls
   Three children visiting an English castle look for the owl that graces the gardens at dusk each day. When the creature is injured, the children go to great pains to try to save its life. Schindler uses the real Sissinghurst as his model. K–4.
   Target Activity: "Weights and Measures"
   Mark wingspans of various owl species on a blackboard by drawing horizontal lines. Provide a step stool so children can spread their arms and compare their own "wingspans" with those of the owls. To show how little these powerful predators weigh, set up a table with a scale, several plastic bags, and some easily measured material, such as dried beans. Have children compile a list of owl weights and fill the bags with equivalent amounts — three pounds for the great horned owl, for example. Relate the weights to the wingspans and discuss how lightweight large wings enable the owl to flap less, fly quietly, and hunt effectively. Finally, on a large sheet of paper, mark the degrees of a circle from 0 to 360. Highlight the 180 and 270 degree marks, which indicate the maximum range of motion of an owl's neck to the left and right. Have children stand in the center of the circle facing zero and mark their own ranges of motion.

35 Steig, William (1986). *Brave Irene.* Illustrated by the author. New York: Farrar, Straus & Giroux.
   Environmental Focus: Feeling the effects of nature's snowstorm
   Irene's mother, a dressmaker, is ill and cannot deliver a ball gown that she has sewn for the duchess to wear that evening. Irene volunteers to take the gown to the duchess despite a fierce snowstorm. A series of obstacles almost prevents Irene from fulfilling her mission — the box is blown from her arms,

Realistic Contemporary Fiction

the dress blows away, and she is nearly buried alive when she falls off a cliff. But Irene perseveres and the gown is delivered to a very grateful duchess. Irene is a plucky character who does not give up when obstacles seem overwhelming. She trudges on, thinking of her mother's face and how unhappy the duchess will be if she doesn't get her dress. She triumphs in the end, inspiring the reader. 1–3.

Target Activity: "Facing a Fierce Snowstorm"

Tell children that Irene's mother cannot fully appreciate the errand that Irene successfully completed in face of the fierce storm unless her mother hears every detail of that very difficult accomplishment. Ask the children to work with partners. Ask one partner to play the part of Irene and tell the many things that happened as she tried to deliver the dress. Encourage "Irene" to share her feelings of frustration along the way as well as her feeling of accomplishment when she arrives at the house of the duchess. Allow the child playing the part of the mother to ad-lib the feelings and the reactions that the proud mother might have made. Then have children trade roles. Finally, several partners may volunteer to present their role plays in front of the total group.

Optional Activity: "Describing a Snowstorm"

Arrange for children to write to a class of children in another part of the country. If you live in a part of the country that has no snow, for example, make sure that the class you choose lives in an area where there are frequent snowstorms. If you live in an area that has snow, have children write to a class that has never seen snow.

After initial introductions, have the focus of the letter be on the topic of snow. Have children summarize the book *Brave Irene* for their pen-pals and then either ask questions they may have about how snow and snowstorms affect their lives or describe snow for the pen-pal. When the letters have been exchanged with the pen pals, discuss how what the children have shared relates to the positive and negative features of snow.

36 Stolz, Mary (1993). *Say Something.* Illustrated by the author. London: Hamish Hamilton Children's Books.

Environmental Focus: Showing an appreciation for nature with language

Enjoying the sights of nature, a young boy and his father pass the time pleasantly as they play a descriptive game while fishing from a rowboat. They take turns and one of them names something and the other describes it. For instance, the father says, "A cave is ..." and the other replies, "A place to get lost in and a place to find your way out." 1–3.

Grades K–3

Target Activity: "A Descriptive Dialogue Game about Nature"

With children, continue this descriptive game of dialogue about the way we can see things and about looking closely at nature to show our appreciation of its wonder and about our part in nature's cycle of things. Consider beginning with: A fish is ...; a tree is ...; and a flower is ...

37 Tresselt, Alvin (1965). *Hide and Seek Fog.* Illustrated by Roger Duvoisin. New York: Lothrop, Lee & Shepard.

Environmental Focus: Recognizing different types of weather

When a fog settles in for three days, it affects the people and their daily activities in different ways. For examples, the fishermen and their lobster boats are kept tied to the wharf, the sailors fold up the sails on the sailboats, and vacationing grownups complain about their vacations being "ruined." Surprisingly, it is the children who enjoy the shadowy and fog-bound days the most by playing hide-and-seek in the gray mist until the sun's warm rays burn off the thick cover. K–2.

Target Activity: "Effects of Fog and Effects of Sun"

Invite children to draw illustrations about fog and sun on both sides of a sheet of art paper. On one side, ask the children to draw sketches of what they would like to do most of all on a sunny day and then, on the other side, draw sketches of what it would look like to do their favorite activity on a foggy day. Discuss with children the reasons for fog and point out weather conditions when fog would be most likely. Ask children to sign their drawings and show and tell about them to the whole group. Display the drawings in a book entitled, "A Foggy Day/A Sunny Day" and place it in a book corner for future browsing.

38 Udry, Janice May (1959). *The Moon Jumpers.* Illustrated by Maurice Sendak. New York: Harper and Brothers.

Environmental Focus: Fostering an appreciation for the differences between day and night

A summer day becomes a new and different environment at night and the children play as shadows fall and darkness comes. Playing, the children imagine they are "moon jumpers" and twirl and prance and dance in the moonlight as the moon "grows" larger and rises in the sky. They dance as the moonfish, frogs, and moths come out. The most challenging play of all is trying to catch the fleeting moonbeams. When it is time to go to bed, the "jumpers" become "just" children once more who eagerly look forward to the next evening and another night of "moonjumping."

Realistic Contemporary Fiction

Target Activity: "A Nocturnal Animal"
Write on the board the term "nocturnal" and explain to children that this word means that the animal is active during the night and sleeps during the day. Explain that a bat is one such animal and ask children to share if they have ever seen a bat (or another nocturnal animal).

Gather magazines such as *Ranger Rick*, *Cricket*, and *Geo World* that have articles and pictures of bats. For children interested further in this topic, encourage them to build a "bat box" where bats can build their nests. For instructions, send $1.00 to:

National Wildlife Federation
Ranger Rick Magazine
8925 Leesburg Pike
Vienna, VA 22184

For more information about bats, have children write to:

Bat Conservation International
P. O. Box 162603
Austin, TX 78716

39 Wilson, Bob (1983). *Stanley Bagshaw and the Twenty-Two Ton Whale*. Illustrated by the author. London: Hamish Hamilton Children's Books.

Environmental Focus: Observing nature during a nature walk

Stanley Bagshaw lives with his Grandma in the north of England where "it's boring and slow." One day, as he goes out for a nature walk with his friend Edward by the Grub Street Canal, Stanley happens upon a whale who is on his way to the Arctic and has "come way off his track." Stan and Edward lead him to the boatyard where he will have room to turn around. At the boatyard, however, there is an annual fishing contest. When the fishermen see the whale they become quite excited and want to catch him with their bait, but Edward explains that whales eat only plankton. The whale turns around and heads back toward the North Pole. K–3.

Target Activity: "Echolocation Game"

Discuss this humorous story and what children learned about what whales eat. Explain that light does not travel well under water but sound does. Some whales have learned to find their food using their sense of hearing rather than their sense of sight. Therefore the whale sends out a sound and when the sound hits a food source, it bounces back to the whale. The whale can tell how far away the source is by noting how long it takes for the sound to travel back to it. By using this technique, called "echolocation," whales can find

Grades K–3

plankton and avoid dangerous places (like the Grub Street Canal!). Have six children form a circle with two children in the middle of the circle. One child in the middle will be the whale, who is blindfolded and has a rattle; the other child will be the prey, who is not blindfolded but also has a rattle. The "whale" shakes its rattle and the prey must shake back. It is the whale's job to locate the prey by heading towards the sound. Each round lasts about three minutes, or until the whale touches its prey.

40 Yashima, Taro (1955). *Crow Boy.* Illustrated by the author. New York: Viking.

Environmental Focus: Acquiring knowledge of nature

A small Asian boy, Chibi, feels isolated at school and spends his time looking at the ceiling, his desk, or out the window. Every day he walks miles to school and notices what is around him. He has six years of perfect attendance and receives attention from a new teacher, Mr. Isobe, who recognizes Chibi's knowledge of nature and discovers that he can imitate the voices of crows. Chibi does so with other students in the school talent show. With this, he earns the respect of others and himself and is nick-named "Crow Boy." K–2.

Target Activity: "Acquiring Knowledge of Nature"

To collect evidence about the ways Crow Boy acquired his knowledge of nature, review the story again with the children and have them look at the illustrations closely. Discuss the following with the children:

1. What evidence can be found about the ways that Crow Boy acquired knowledge about nature? How did this knowledge make him special? List on the board.

2. Invite the students to draw a picture of Crow Boy showing what he knew about nature. After the drawings are completed, ask the children to team up as partners and talk about what they drew with each other. Display the illustrations in the classroom.

41 Yashima, Taro (1967). *Seashore Story.* Illustrated by the author. New York: Viking.

Environmental Focus: Appreciating the unique nature of the sea and the shore

In this gentle story-within-a-story, a group of children from a ballet school camp in the sand dunes on an island on the southern tip of Japan. The tranquillity of the seashore reminds them of the familiar story of Urashima who saved the life of a wounded turtle and lived in a beautiful place under

Realistic Contemporary Fiction

the sea, almost forgetting about those he loved. When he returned, his family was gone and no one even remembered them. The ballet school children discuss the veracity of this tale as the breeze blows the children's voices into the sky and "even the clouds seem to be listening." K–3.

Target Activity: "A Place Where City Noises Never Come at All"

The author describes this quiet seashore as "a seashore where city noises never come at all" (p. 1, unpaged). Ask children what they think is special about such a place. Discuss the significance of nature reserves and other protected environments so that the children and THEIR children will always have places that they can go to escape the "city noises." For children in grades K–2 who are interested in further exploring nature outdoors, introduce your favorite video about being a safe camper or introduce "Happy Campers with Miss Shirley and Friends" (Kids Express Co., 11176 Springfield, MO 65808 [1992]) and tell children to listen to discover ways to be safe and handle emergencies on a camp-out.

Optional Activity: "Save the Turtles"

Like the author Taro Yashima, children can get involved with saving the lives of wounded or endangered turtles. Information about doing so may be obtained from:

> The Center for Marine Conservation
> 1725 De Sales Street, NW
> Washington, DC 20036

A sea turtle coloring book is also available at the above address if you enclose $1.00.

42 Yashima, Taro (1958). *Umbrella*. Illustrated by the author. New York: Viking.

Environmental Focus: Appreciating the rain

On her birthday, three-year-old Momo receives a gift of red rubber boots and an umbrella and she waits for the rain to come. When it rains, Momo wears her boots and carries her umbrella as she walks to nursery school. Using her gifts makes the day an exciting one for Momo: she is allowed to walk to school without holding anyone's hand. Pre–1.

Target Activity: "Rain Drops as Silver Nails"

Ask children how they feel about rain. Have they ever felt unhappy about rain when it kept them from doing a favorite outdoor activity? Introduce children to the idea that small things in the environment can take on a new significance through the words of a poet and introduce a poem about rain called "Rain Song" by David McCord in *One at a Time* (Little, Brown, 1980).

It begins with the words, "The rain is driving silver nails / into the shingles overhead." Follow up with McCord's "Summer Shower" and its opening of "Window window window pane. / Let it let it let it rain."

Optional Activity: "Where Does Rain Come From?"

Invite a weather forecaster or meteorologist to come and speak to the class. Beforehand, discuss the following questions with children. For those questions to which they do not know the answers, encourage them to ask the invited speaker:

- Where does rain come from?
- Why is rainfall different in different places?
- How do mountains affect rainfall?
- Are there two cities that are both in mountains that have very different rainfalls?
- How do weather forecasters know what the weather is going to be?

43 Zion, Eugene (1959). *The Plant Sitter.* Illustrated by Margaret Bloy Graham. New York: Harper and Row.

Environmental Focus: Appreciating and caring for house plants

Since Tommy's family had no vacation planned, he decided to offer his services as a "plant sitter." He takes very good care of his customers' plants, giving sun to those requiring sun, and providing a shady spot to those needing shade, and watering all the plants according to their individual needs. The plants flourish, but a bit too much. After he has a nightmare about the plants overtaking the house, he goes to the library and does some research. He learns how to prune his plants and he plants all the cuttings in little flower pots and gives them to neighborhood children. When Tommy's plant sitting is over, his father decides he misses all the greenery, and takes the family to the country for a surprise vacation. K–3.

Target Activity: "Growing and Caring for a Plant"

Bring in a plant for the class to grow as Tommy did. Have children find out what the plant needs to grow by interviewing a nursery worker, e.g., how much shade / sun, water, fertilizer, pruning, etc. Have pairs of children care for the plant each week. Ask children to make crayon drawings of their observations of the plant's growth on a weekly basis. When the plant is ready for trimming, allow children to plant the cuttings in paper cups full of earth, just as Tommy did. When the plant has reached maturity, help children to transplant it in a safe place in the school yard where they can continue to care for it.

Realistic Contemporary Fiction

44 Zolotow, Charlotte (1980). *Flocks of Birds.* Illustrated by Ruth Lercher Bornstein. New York: Crowell.

Environmental Focus: Imaging flocks of birds as part of nature

The little girl in this gentle story is not tired yet and asks her mother for "something good to think about" until she can fall asleep. Her mother suggests that she think of "flocks of birds flying south." When the child asks her to be more specific, the mother paints an eloquent picture of soaring birds in flight across mountains and valleys "like a pool of black ink." She presents an irresistible image of flocks of birds as part of city life and country life, enriching the lives of girls and boys like the readers. 2–3.

Target Activity: "Flocks of Birds"

Reread the text, this time asking children to listen for specific imagery so that children can draw pictures of flocks of birds in various places in the environments that are mentioned in the book: Flocks of Birds ...

1. "over mountains where the trees are yellow and crimson and brown, and only the pines are green" (p. 12).

2. "over rivers where the boats cut choppy little white-edged waves into the windy water" (p. 13).

3. "through the long purple and pink clouds of the sunset and through the blackness of the night" (p. 14).

Optional Activity: "Bird Homes"

Ask each child to draw a picture of where he or she lives — or to draw a picture of the place where a person they know lives. Ask children to include in their drawings the things they need to live where they do, for example, a place to cook and keep food, a place to sleep, a neighborhood.

Once the drawings are finished, have a discussion with children about what they drew. Ask them to point out the things they need to live that they included in their drawings. Make a "gallery of homes" out of the drawings. Point out to children that everyone has a place to live.

Ask the children to close their eyes and imagine a bird's home. Show the children pictures of different places that birds live. Discuss the differences and similarities between human homes and bird homes. Talk about the things that both birds and humans need in their environment — food, water, shelter, and space in which to live that is arranged in a way so the bird or human can survive. Summarize the discussion by emphasizing that although the "homes" of the two species are different, both humans and birds need a home. Talk about the fact that a home is actually bigger than a house; it is more like a neighborhood. For birds, we call the neighborhood where all their survival needs are met a "habitat." People leave home to get food, and birds also have to go out of their places of shelter to get the things they need to live.

Grades K–3

45 Zolotow, Charlotte (1980). *Say It!* Illustrated by James Stevenson. New York: Greenwillow.

Environmental Focus: Vicariously experiencing a windy autumn day

This warm story celebrates the love between a mother and her daughter as they take a walk on a golden, windy autumn day. It also celebrates the beauty of trees in the fall when they dazzle with different brilliant colors and then their leaves crunch under our feet. The two walk through a meadow, a field, and finally down to a brook bubbling over mossy green rocks. Finally, the mother says, "I love you!" to the child who has been asking her mother to "Say It!" Before that, all the mother could do was exclaim about the overwhelming beauty of the day. K–2.

Target Activity: "Guided Imagery Nature Walk"

Discuss with children how the mother in this story was really appreciating the natural beauty of the world around her. Have children close their eyes and lead them on a guided visualization of a nature walk in their area in the current season. Then ask them to turn to a neighbor in the room and recall the walk in their own words, adding their own feeling and exclamations as the mother in the story did. Finally, encourage children to show their visualized walks pictorially, using crayons, chalk, water colors, or other available media.

46 Zolotow, Charlotte (1992). *The Seashore Book.* Illustrated by Wendell Manor. New York: HarperCollins.

Environmental Focus: Recognizing what the seashore environment is like

A mother tries to explain to her child what the seashore is like. They live in the mountains and the young boy can only experience the seashore vicariously through her description. Mother describes a wonderful day at the seashore — the "swishing sound" of waves and oyster shells that are "crusty gray outside and smooth, pearly pink on the inside." Between the mother's evocative description and the beautiful paintings of the seashore, readers who have never been to the seashore will get the idea; those who have been there will actually be able to smell the salty air and feel the hot sand on their toes. 1–3.

Target Activity: "At the Seashore"

Ask children to close their eyes and lead them through a guided imagery where they look for shells, chase waves, wade in the water, and build sand castles while they can feel the hot sun, the gentle sea breeze, and the sand between their toes. Ask them to listen for the swishing waves and the cries of the seagulls. Have them open their eyes and tell a neighbor about their day at the seashore. Have them to finish the sentence frame "One thing I appreciate about the seashore is_____."

Folk Literature

Folk literature — the narratives that originated orally and have been handed down in diverse cultures from generation to generation through the years — come in various forms. Many folktales relate to the environment and include cumulative tales, the "how and why" tales, the talking animal tales, noodlehead stories, and the "wonder" tales with magic and super beings. Several stories that relate to the environment are quite direct, with episodic actions that move the plot along quickly. An example is a cumulative tale such as *Bringing the Rain to Kapiti Plain* (Dial, 1981), written by Verna Aardema and illustrated by Beatriz Vidal, wherein repetition of details builds up to the climax of how the drought ends. This book can be used with children to underscore the importance of conserving one of our most important natural resources, water.

In another example, *Why the Sun and the Moon Live in the Sky: An African Folktale*, the "how and why" tale explains the phenomena of the sun and moon in the manner of all such tales, relating the traits, characteristics, or phenomena of people, animals, and natural happenings. In *Tiddalick the Frog* and other talking animal tales, the animals act and talk like humans. In the Australian Aborigine tale, Noyang, the eel, makes Tiddalick release the water the land needs.

If the folktale is a story with a character who acts as a silly noodlehead such as Iktomi is portrayed in *Iktomi and the Boulder: A Plains Indian Story*, the emphasis is on humor as the character interacts with nature. By contrast, realistic "fairy tale–type" stories portray a realistic setting and the characters suggest to children that the story might REALLY have happened. The additional folk literature discussed in the following section conveys a sense of "what has been" for early people, what is still cared about, and what might be valued in the future.

Grades K–3

47 Belting, Natalia, editor (1962). *The Sun Is a Golden Earring.* Illustrated by Bernard Bryson. New York: Holt, Rinehart and Winston.

Environmental Focus: Appreciating and expressing associations and comparisons found in nature

Though out of print, this book can be found in a library's Caldecott Medal book collection. It is a collection of folk sayings from around the world about the theme of nature's phenomena. Traditional quotes about clouds, lightning, the moon, a rainbow, the sun, stars, sky, thunder, and the wind are included in the collection. The author connects the phenomena with important elements in the lives of people from different cultures. 3.

Target Activity: "Points of View about Nature"

Introduce the idea that elements in nature can be seen from a different point of view through the words of a poet, and introduce poems about the elements from *One at a Time* (Little, Brown, 1980) by David McCord. Some suggestions and opening words to read aloud are:

Nature's Element	Poem
moon	Watching the Moon (p. 72) "September evenings such as these / The moon hides early in the trees"
rainbow	The Rainbow (p. 11) "The rainbow arches in the sky, / But in the earth it ends / And if you ask the reason why, / They'll tell you 'That depends.'"
sun	The Firetender (p. 34) "Each morning when the dawn returns, / And hills and trees and fields and ferns / Are grateful in the gaining light, / He rises from the dead of night / And rakes the star-coals up in the sky /"
stars	The Star in the Pail (p. 13) "I took the pail for water when the sun was high / And left it in the shadow of the barn nearby /"
sky	Take Sky (p. 125) "Now think of words, Take sky / And ask yourself just why — / Like sun, moon, star, and cloud — / It sounds so well out loud, /"
wind	The Wind (p. 79) "Wind in the garden, / Wind on the hill, / Wind I-am-blowing, / Never be still."

48 Carreno, Mada, reteller (1987). *El Viaje del joven Matsua (The Travels of the Youth Matsua).* Illustrated by Gerado Suzan. Mexico City: Trillas.

Folk Literature

Environmental Focus: Understanding the effects of drought

When Matsua and his family leave their land because there is no water, they travel to another place and wonder if the Tarahumara will receive them well. As they grow closer, Matsua discovers a young Tarahumara trapped on a cliff and threatened by a large vulture. Matsua's family is welcomed by the family of the boy Matsua rescues. 1–3.

Target Activity: "Similarities of Drought Situations"

With the children, compare the effects of the drought in this story to the effects of the drought in *Bringing the Rain to Kapiti Plain: A Nandi Tale*. What do the two drought situations have in common? Ask children to outline the shapes of their right and left hands on paper. Do the same on the board. In the outline of one hand, write the words "Matsua's Family," and in the outline of the other, write "Herdsman." Under each heading, write the words that identify the effects of the drought on each. Discuss with the whole group each of the effects of a drought as they are identified and written. Then, have children trade papers with study partners and discuss what was written. Finally, brainstorm some ways that the Kapitian children could have helped their tribe conserve water. How are the brainstormed ideas the same and different from ways ALL human beings everywhere should be conserving our scarce natural resources such as water?

49 Dayrell, Elpphinstone (1968). *Why the Sun and the Moon Live in the Sky: An African Folktale.* Illustrated by Blair Lent. Boston: Houghton Mifflin.

Environmental Focus: Learning about early people's beliefs about the sun and water

When the Sun and his wife, the Moon, ask the water why water never visited the sun at his house, water says that his friend's house is too small for water and all of his people. The Sun builds a huge house and water arrives at the house of the Sun, but as more and more of water's relatives flow into the house, the Sun and the Moon are forced to move up higher and higher until they float out into the sky. This is a Nigerian tale from the Efik-Ibibio people. 1–3.

Target Activity: "Nature Poems"

Introduce the idea that some traditional African tales and poetry are related to the people's close relationship with nature and are part of their daily vocabulary. Some of the poems are sung and chanted and danced to in everyday life and are found in *A Crocodile Has Me by the Leg: African Poems* (Walker and Co., 1967) edited by Leonard W. Doob. Read aloud the poems that reflect the people's relationship with nature:

Grades K–3

1. "This Little Cloud" is a poem that is a plea: "Give us water, / Our hearts are dry, O Lord."

2. In "We Must Overcome the East Wind," the words also cry out for water, "we crave rain, / Let showers pour, / Let rain fall; / If rain comes, then all is well."

3. The poem "You Who Cultivate Fields" is a recognition of the value of the harvest with the words, "your merit is great, / Wealth flows from your fingers."

4. The poem "Morning Prayer" recognizes the greatness of a mountain with "O Great Mountain, you chief. / Whom we live beside."

5. The poem "Dance of the Animals" shows respect for the animals with, "I throw myself to the left. / I turn myself to the right. / I am the fish / Who glides in the water, who flies, / Who twists himself, who leaps. / Everything lives, everything dances, everything sings."

6. The poem "We Mold a Pot" is one of the songs of the young girls who say, "We mold a pot as our mothers did. / The pot, where is the pot? / The pot, it is here. / We mold the pot as our mothers did."

50 DePaola, Tomie, reteller (1983). *The Legend of the Bluebonnet.* Illustrated by the reteller. New York: Scholastic.

Environmental Focus: Understanding the belief of the Comanche people about the importance of flowers

In this retold Comanche legend, a drought and famine have killed the mother, father and grandparents of She-Who-Is-Alone, a small girl. All she has left is a warrior doll that her mother once made for her. One evening, the shaman of the camp tells his people that the famine is the result of the people becoming selfish. They must make a sacrifice of the most valued possession among them and life will be restored. No one volunteers a valued possession except She-Who-Is-Alone, who offers her warrior doll. Deep in the night she makes a burnt offering of the doll, and then scatters its ashes over the fields below. Where the ashes have fallen, the ground becomes covered with bluebonnets. The Comanche people take the flowers as a sign of forgiveness from the Great Spirits. From that day on, the little girl is known as One-Who-Dearly-Loved-Her-People. 2–3.

Target Activity: "A Famine Legend for Today"

Have children rewrite *The Legend of Bluebonnet*, superimposing themselves as a character with a prized possession related to a "famine" in today's times. Tell the children:

1. Describe the famine. Tell what you say when you offer a prized possession as a sacrifice to end the famine.

2. How does the character feel? Describe the night on the mountain. What happens as a result of the character's sacrifice?

3. How does the character feel about saving others? What has the character learned from the experience?

51 DePaola, Tomie, reteller (1988). *The Legend of the Indian Paintbrush.* Illustrated by the reteller. New York: Putnam Group.

Environmental Focus: Developing an appreciation for flowers and colors of the desert

This is the story of Little Gopher, who cannot be like other children, but who, through his art, has a special gift for his people. Loyal Little Gopher finds that his place among his people is to paint their deeds to be remembered always. He is lonely, but faithful and true, and is rewarded with magical brushes left on a hillside. They hold colors and allow him to paint his vision of the evening sky. Discarded, they take root and multiply and bloom in colors of red, orange, and yellow. K–2.

Target Activity: "Colors for Paintbrushes"

Discuss the colors used for painting and invite children to see the ways primary colors turn into other colors with the overhead projector, a clear glass or plastic container, water, and drops of food coloring. Drops of red and yellow food coloring in the water in the container are swirled and the overhead projects the mingling as the colors turn into orange. Encourage children to use the colors of red, orange, yellow, and other shades to create their own visions of the environment — the evening sky or other visions. Help children to compare the colors in their paintings with the colors found in nature.

52 Esbensen, Barbara Juster (1988). *The Star Maiden.* Illustrated by Helen K. Davie. Boston: Little, Brown.

Environmental Focus: Appreciating the importance of nature as recorded in folk literature

This is an explanatory tale describing the genesis of a flower that originated with the Obijway (Chippewa) in the north lake country. A star maiden watches the earth and wants to make her home with the tribe who prepare to welcome her. The rose on the hillside where she first comes to rest is too far from the village and a flower on the prairie is too near the trampling feet of buffalo. Finally, she finds the peaceful surface of a lake and calls her sisters down to live with her where they can be seen today as water lilies. 1–3.

Grades K–3

Target Activity: "Appreciating the Peacefulness of Nature"

Have the students get together with partners to tell one another about a time when they found a natural setting peaceful to their own natures. Have them describe the setting in detail. Ask them to sketch something they remember about the peaceful scene and tell one another about their drawings. Ask them to tell why they think that nature can have a peaceful effect on them. Ask them to describe a setting in nature that was not peaceful. What was going on in the nonpeaceful setting?

53 Gerstein, Mordecai (1993). *The Story of May.* Illustrated by the author. New York: HarperCollins.

Environmental Focus: Fostering an appreciation for the beauty of the seasons

The colors of earth tones and sky tones guide a reader to the story of May, a fanciful character and a "little month of a girl." May is the daughter of April, an earth mother reminiscent of the Greek goddess Demeter, and of December, an earth father whom she seeks. May searches for him through the calendar and meets her relatives — Uncle July, Grandmother November, Aunt February and Cousin March and discovers their seasonal nature. May finds her way back to her mother after her search for her family "roots." Pre–2.

Target Activity: "A Monthly Calendar Reflects Nature's Seasons"

With students review the months of the year and discuss their "natures" as they were personified in the story about May. Relate the nature of the seasons to ways the seasons help or hinder life in the environment. Brainstorm ideas with children and write their suggestions on the board or on an overhead transparency:

                  helps   hinders

1. Spring
2. Summer
3. Fall
4. Winter

Interested children may study folktale origins of the seasons with stories from different countries. Related readings can include any of the following:

Greece:

Hodges, M. *Persephone and the Springtime.* Illustrated. Little Brown, 1973. Greek story explaining the change of seasons. 5 up.

Proddow, P., translator. *Demeter and Persephone.* Illustrated B.Cooney. Doubleday, 1972. Demeter, the mother who caused plants to grow, mourns for her daughter, Persephone. 5 up.

Tomaino. S. F. *Persephone, Bringer of Spring.* Illustrated A. Forberg. Crowell, 1971. Persephone is bound to Hades for four months each year. 5 up.

Italy:
McDermott, G. *Daughter of Earth: A Roman Myth.* Delacorte, 1984. The illustrations resemble the ancient art work of Romans. 5 up.

North America:
Leland, C. G. "How Glooskap Found the Summer." *The Algonquin Legends of New England.* Houghton Mifflin, 1984. 4–6.
Toye, W. *How Summer Came to Canada.* Illustrated E. Cleaver. Walck, 1969. Glooskap saves his people from Winter and persuades Summer to stay for part of the year. 5 up.

54 Goble, Paul, reteller (1988). *Her Seven Brothers.* Illustrated by the reteller. New York: Bradbury Press.
Environmental Focus: Appreciating the beauty of the constellations

A lonely Indian girl makes clothing decorated with porcupine quills for seven brothers she has never seen, and after many months, she travels north with her mother to find the seven brothers. When she finds the trail she wants, the girl says goodbye to her mother with the words, "Soon you will see me again with my brothers; everyone will know and love us!" In the land of pines, she finds the tipi of the brothers, gives them their clothing, and is looked after well by the brothers. One day, the chief of the Buffalo nation wants the sister, and when the brothers refuse to let her go, the chief threatens to return with the whole Buffalo nation and kill them. Later, a shaking of the earth announces the rumbling of the Buffalo people stampeding toward the tipi. When the youngest brother shoots an arrow up into the air, a pine tree appears and grows upward as fast as the flight of the arrow. The girl and the brothers climb up just as the chief of the Buffalo strikes the tree a mighty blow and the tree starts to topple over. The youngest brother shoots arrow after arrow into the sky and the tree continues to grow taller and taller until they are all far away up among the stars. There, they jump down from the branches onto the prairies of the world above the Earth. The girl and her brothers are still there and can be seen as the Big Dipper. If one looks quite closely, one of the stars is near a tiny star that represents the little boy walking with his sister, who is never lonely now. K–3.

Target Activity: "Nature in Cheyenne Designs"
In the Cheyenne designs (circa 1900), one sees animals, birds, butterflies,

and flowers. Since these living creatures share the Earth with humans, the creatures are always included in the designs. Sometimes two of each are drawn, or to show abundance, many are drawn. Ask children what designs they would make for a tipi of their own. Would their designs include the members of the Buffalo nation, the faithful dogs, the nearby deer, the porcupine "who climbs trees closest to Sun himself?" Engage them in drawing a sketch of the design and showing it to others. Invite them to discuss the designs with partners and explain their reasons for drawing what they did. What meaning does the design have for the young artist?

55 Goble, Paul, reteller (1988). *Iktomi and the Boulder: A Plains Indian Story.* Illustrated by the reteller. New York: Orchard Books/Watts.

Environmental Focus: Understanding the Plains Indians' use of humor when trying to outwit a natural force

The vain Iktomi (eek toe me), the Plains Indian who gets into the worst kind of trouble, has overdressed for his journey. When he grows too warm, he offers his blanket as a gift to a boulder. When it begins to rain, Iktomi pretends the gift was only a loan. While Iktomi congratulates himself on his foresight in bringing the blanket, the boulder comes to reclaim the gift. Iktomi tries to elude the boulder, but it pins his legs. As the moon rises, bats appear and Iktomi tricks them into attacking the boulder. The bats break the boulder into small stones, which is why bats have flat faces and why there are rocks scattered over the Great Plains. Ink and watercolor illustration show movement. K–3.

Target Activity: "An Indian Trickster Character Interacts with Nature"

Discuss the background information in the foreword about Indian trickster characters and Iktomi. Young children enjoy the humor in this trickster tale of Iktomi, the Plains Indian, and they laugh at his vanity; he is always overdressed. Point out that the book has large type and an informal narrative voice with asides from the storyteller and the character, Iktomi. Dark print tells children what happens; light print gives asides from the teller e.g., That's not true, is it? and invites comments from the audience. Invite children to describe other trickster characters they know about from other stories. Build a chart of information to show what the children know about this type of character in literature and ways tricksters interact with nature.

Folk Literature

56 Hodges, Margaret (1964). *The Wave.* Illustrated by Blair Lent. Boston: Houghton Mifflin.

Environmental Focus: Recognizing cause-and-effect in nature's signals

In Japan, on a mountainside of rice fields overlooking a village below, Tada and his wise grandfather, Ojiisan, enjoy the respect of the villagers who come to the elderly man for advice and guidance. The people are gathered on the seashore to celebrate a plentiful rice harvest when they feel a mild earthquake rocking the village and the mountain. Ojiisan, far above them, senses a post-quake danger and alerts the people by setting fire to his rice fields. Seeing the fire, the people rush up the mountainside to help him put out the fire, but they become angry when they discover he started it himself and burned his own fields. Suddenly, the villagers see a giant tidal wave destroy the village below them and swiftly carry away bits and pieces of their belongings. Eventually, the people rebuild the village, re-till the rice fields, and erect a temple to honor Ojiisan and memorialize his self-sacrifice. K–3.

Target Activity: "A Moment in Nature with Nature Poetry"

Introduce children in grade 3 and older to more of nature's effects with the book, *Zen ABC* (Charles E. Tuttle, 1993) by Amy Zerner and Jessie Spicer Zerner. This book reflects the rich sensitivity of Zen, the experience of "no" thing. Each letter of the alphabet has a Zen-related word described by a haiku (nature poetry), a koan (unanswerable question, such as "What is the sound of one hand clapping?"), or a phrase from the classical literature of Zen. For example, a listener can be guided to imagine the cadence of the rain with this haiku: "Spring rain on my roof / begins to drum; / Drips from the willow, petals / from the plum." A reader senses that the slumber of a butterfly is disturbed in "The butterfly / Sleeps well / Perched on the / Temple Bell / Till, clang, it rings." A reader also senses the calmness of Zen meditation with "Sitting quietly, doing nothing / Spring comes, grass grows of itself."

57 Kimmel, Eric A., reteller (1992). *Anansi Goes Fishing.* Illustrated by Janet Stevens. New York: Holiday House.

Environmental Focus: Recognizing how a "why tale" explains the beginning of spider webs

In this West African tale, Anansi, a trickster, wants to trick Turtle, who wears a flowered shirt, sunglasses, and carries a boom box, into doing the work of catching a fish. Anansi wants the fish for himself. However, Turtle is clever and divides the work. Starting each new task, Turtle asks Anansi if he wants to do the work or "to get tired." Of course, Anansi doesn't want to get tired, so he chooses to do the work of making the net, setting the net, catching the fish and cooking it. This allows Turtle to lounge under his umbrella, listen to his music, munch on chips, and drink a cool drink as he "gets tired." Then Turtle asks Anansi if he wants to eat the fish or "get full" and only after Turtle has eaten the fish does Anansi see that he, the trickster, has been tricked. Angry Anansi asks for Justice at the Justice Tree but Warthog dismisses the case, leaving Anansi only with the knowledge of weaving, something he learned while making the fishing net. So Anansi teaches his friends weaving and they teach their friends and "to this day, wherever you find spiders, you will find their nets. They are called spider webs." K–3.

Target Activity: "What Can You Find in Anansi's Natural Environment?"

Review the illustrations with children and mention that animals are hiding in the watery, African setting. The artist has hidden small bush deer and other African animals who watch the different actions of Anansi and Turtle throughout the story. Invite children to closely observe the environment in the illustrations and "find the animal" on each colorful page. Additionally, discuss the comparisons that are seen in the behavior of Anansi and Turtle.

Optional Activity: "Observing a Spider"

Send pairs of children out to a nearby wildlife area, with supervision, to collect spiders in plastic jars. Caution the students not to harm the spiders. Tell children they are going to be like good scientists — carefully observing wildlife with as little impact as possible.

On a ditto master, write the following questions for children to answer as they observe the spiders. Give a copy to each pair of children and allow plenty of space for their answers:

- How many legs does the spider have?
- How many eyes does it have?
- Do you see a mouth or lips?
- How does the spider move?
- Is the spider the same color all over?
- What is attractive/not attractive about your spider?
- Where did you find your spider?
- What shapes/designs of webs did you see?
- What does the spider eat?
- What were some of the interesting things you observed about the spider?
- Did you think there were so many interesting things about a spider? In what ways would another spider/insect/small bug be as interesting?

Folk Literature

58 Lottridge, Celia Barker, reteller (1990). *The Name of the Tree.* Illustrated by Ian Wallace. New York: McElderry Books/ Macmillan.

Environmental Focus: Problem-solving in a drought

When a drought settles on an African plain, animals search for food and find a tree with every fruit imaginable. This Bantu folktale tells that the animals must learn the name of the tree before it will surrender its bounty. Muted grays and greens in illustrations show the dry land and hot African sun. K–3.

Target Activity: "Problem-solving: The Importance of Water"

Explore what the Nandi culture and Bantu culture in Africa have in common with our own; discuss our reliance on water and the resiliency of people (or animals posing as people in stories) when they are faced with this problem. Compare the solution in this story to the one in *Bringing the Rain to Kapiti Plain: A Nandi Tale* and identify the importance of water to all people.

Optional Activity: "Avoiding a Drought"

Place a rain gauge on your school grounds and measure the actual amounts of rain daily. Find out what would constitute a "drought" in your area and find out the last time there was such a problem in your area.

Create a poster campaign to alert the children in the school to the consequences of wasting water with or without a drought situation. Brainstorm some changes that people could make in their lifestyle that would help to prevent a water shortage, such as:

- Choose a brief shower instead of a bath;
- Turn off the water when you brush your teeth;
- Fix leaky faucets; and
- Water the lawn only when necessary.

59 Luenn, Nancy, reteller (1993). *Song for the Ancient Forest.* Illustrated by Jill Kastner. New York: Atheneum.

Environmental Focus: Appreciating the concern for nature in folk literature

In prehistoric times, Raven has a bad dream about the destruction of the old prehistoric forests. He tries, mostly in vain, to get someone to help and to listen to his melodious message. K–3.

Target Activity: "A Problem in Prehistory Continues in the Present"

With the children, discuss Raven's dilemma and relate the destruction of the old forests that Raven worried about with the present conflict in some communities between people who rely on the trees for their livelihood and people

Grades K–3

who want no trees to be cut. Ask children for suggestions from people they know or have heard about who are listening to "Raven's message" today and write their names on the board.

60 Martin, Rafe, reteller (1993). *The Boy Who Lived with the Seals.* Illustrated by David Shannon. New York: Putnam.
Environmental Focus: Living with nature's creatures
 In this Chinook legend, a young boy disappears and is not found until the following spring when the people see him among the wild seals at the river's mouth. The boy is captured and returned to his parents. His parents teach him their human ways of making carvings and a bow and arrows. But one day he rejoins the seals and asks his parents not to grieve about this. In recognition of where he is, his parents put the box of carving tools into the river. In return, each spring he leaves them a beautifully carved canoe. 1–3.
Target Activity: "Looking at the Art of the Northwest Coast People"
 With children, review the illustrations that show the way the boy's parents accepted his individuality and his love for nature's creatures—the seals. Discuss the title and the meaning it has for the way the Northwest Coast People looked at their artwork. How does their artwork express their profound appreciation for nature?

61 Nunes, Susan (1989). *Tiddalick the Frog.* Illustrated by Ju-Hong Chen. New York: Atheneum.
Environmental Focus: Recognizing the importance of water
 Once upon a time in the Dreamtime, before humans were on the earth, there was a gigantic frog named Tiddalick, who was so huge that his shadow turned day into night, and when he jumped, the ground shook for miles and miles. One morning when he awoke feeling thirsty, he drank all the fresh water in the world. What would happen without fresh water? The land grows hot and dry and the plants all die. All the animals are terribly thirsty. Tiddalick doesn't care and will not release the water until Noyang, the eel, changes the frog's bad mood, and the waters gush forth from his mouth to nourish the earth once more. Derived from the Australian Aborigines. K–3.
Target Activity: "Conserving Water"
 Ask children to imagine what it would be like if, as in the story, their water supply were severely limited and water rationing were necessary. Urge children to act as community council members and decide on a water rationing

Folk Literature

program for their communities. Allow them to make a list of water conservation rules which they can follow, such as taking five-minute showers instead of baths and turning off the faucet as they brush their teeth. Have children create a poster to display the water rules. Award certificates of merit or buttons to those who become exceptional water conservationists.

62 Xiong, Blia, reteller (1989). *Nine-in-One Grr! Grr!* Illustrated by Nancy Hom. Adapted by Cathy Spagnoli. Chicago: Children's Book Press.

Environmental Focus: Explaining a tiger's characteristics through a "why" tale

In this Hmong folktale, the world began when a lonely tiger journeyed to the great god Shao to discover if she will have cubs. Shao says that she will have nine cubs a year if she can remember his words. To remember, the tiger says a memory chant on the way home with the words "nine-in-one one, Grr! Grr!" The Eu bird (black bird) asks Shao to change what he said because if Tiger has nine cubs each year, the tigers will eat all of the Eu birds. Since this cannot be done, the black bird flies to the tiger and substitutes the words "one in nine" altering natural history and the rest of creation. Illustrations have intricate borders and are reminiscent of story stitching or the stories told in needlework. 1–3.

Target Activity: "Black Bird's Problem"

The Eu bird has a problem: if Tiger has nine cubs each year, they will eat all of the birds. Planning ahead about what to do, the bird flies to the tiger (who is trying to remember the magical words of the great god Shao), and interferes with the arrangement of the words by reversing the words "nine in one" to "one in nine." Invite children to discuss the problem faced by the black bird and the way it was solved. Encourage boys and girls to think of other ways the story could have solved the problem for the bird. On the chalkboard, write down the ideas dictated by the children. Ask children to draw scenes of ways the problem could have been solved.

Optional Activity: "Myths About Animals"

Prepare a series of large photos or drawings of a tiger, a black bird, and other different kinds of animals. As you show a picture to children, ask them to take turns saying the first word that enters their mind as they see the picture. Write the name of the animal and the words the children suggest on the board. Ask children to identify the animals that generate a response of dislike or fear, and those that generate mostly a positive response.

Ask the class to choose an animal, such as the tiger, that seems especially

Grades K–3

frightening. Tell children that this animal makes an important contribution to its environment — and that they will find out what that contribution is. On your own or with the help of a local resource person, find out more about the contributions of the animal and report back to the children. Talk about "first impressions" of a frightening animal contrasted with reactions based upon actual knowledge.

Fanciful Fiction

Fanciful fiction — narratives that could not possibly happen in the real world as we know it — can provide not only fundamental environmental truths, but new insights to younger readers. Young readers have several fine books to choose from in this genre, such as *The Tree in the Ancient Forest* by Carol Reed-Jones. Told in the familiar cadence of *The House That Jack Built*, this fanciful tale of a tree also offers a solid ecology lesson on old growth forests.

63 Halsey, Megan (1994). *3 Pandas Counting*. New York: Bradbury.

Environmental Focus: Saving the earth

This counting book is perfect for the budding ecologist. Counting down from 12 to 1, the animals featured are doing something to help save the earth. For example, the alligators carpool, the bears recycle newspapers, and the rhinos use rechargeable batteries. There is also a section in the back of the book with more detailed information about each of the earth-friendly activities mentioned. A portion of the royalties will be donated to Friends of the Earth. K–2.

Target Activity: "Animal Save the Earth Book"

After reading the book aloud to children, ask them to brainstorm some other animals that have not been mentioned in Halsey's book. Write these animals on the blackboard. Ask children to think of some activities these animals might get involved in to help the environment. Use the information in the back of the book to help children get ideas. Have each child write one new page for a new animal counting book, such as one that says, "The cat turns off the tap when she brushes her teeth."

64 Reed-Jones, Carol (1995). *The Tree in the Ancient Forest*. New York: Dawn Publications.

Environmental Focus: Recognizing the interdependence of plants and animals

Grades K–3

Children discover how plants and animals depend on one another in this fanciful story about a majestic Douglas fir tree. Luminous paintings bring the forest to life. Readers will vicariously listen to the brash rat-a-tat-tat of a woodpecker and feel the spongy moss on the forest floor. The brilliant illustrations inspire a reverence for and an understanding of the web of life and help young children appreciate how one break in the web can affect a whole ecosystem. Printed on recycled paper with soy-based ink. K–4.

Target Activity: "Flannel Board Retelling"

Using a flannel board and felt cut-outs of the plants and animals in this story, encourage children to retell the story of the life of the Douglas fir in sequence, pointing out how each plant and animal along the way affects each other plant and animal in some way. Allow one child to manipulate each plant or animal as it is mentioned by a child paraphrasing the story. Do several retellings, changing characters each time.

65 Spinner, Stephanie (1994). *Aliens for Dinner.* New York: Random House.

Environmental Focus: Stopping pollution

A bossy extraterrestrial named Aric has popped out of Richard's fortune cookie with urgent news: a group of pollution-loving aliens named the Dwibs are getting ready to turn planet Earth into a Toxic Waste Theme Park. Their only hope is to incapacitate the invaders with a fatal case of boredomitis at the opening ceremonies for the new recycling plant. Can they find someone really boring in time? The principal of Richard's school may have the answer. Fast-paced hilarity to delight newly-independent readers. 1–4.

Target Activity: "A Toxic Waste Theme Park"

On the blackboard or overhead, write the words "Toxic Waste Theme Park." Ask children to brainstorm some pollution-causing practices that might be highlighted at such a place. Using a large sheet of butcher paper and tempera paints, encourage children to paint scenes depicting people engaged in these various earth-unfriendly activities, making each one an amusement park ride, concession games, or other attraction that one would be likely to see at a theme park. Place the butcher paper across a wall in the back of the classroom and refer to it in a discussion of the dangers of pollution-causing activities.

Historical Fiction

Historical fiction — vignettes of everyday life in various time periods — can cover a wide range of times in ancient history, in the Middle Ages, and in contemporary times, and the settings can include Canada, Latin and Middle America, the United States, and Europe, as well as other parts of the globe. For this section, books have been selected that portray in some way the thoughts, reflections, or memories of children and adults who have worked and played in different time periods as they interacted with nature in their own unique ways.

66 Brenner, Barbara (1978). *Wagon Wheels.* An I CAN READ history book. New York: Harper & Row.

Environmental Focus: Surviving in the wilderness and its harsh winter days

This book has a setting in Kansas in the 1870s and is based upon a true story taken from the diaries of a family of black settlers in the pioneer days. The Muldie boys and their father have traveled the arduous wilderness trail in covered wagons from the east coast to Kansas. The boys' mother died on the trail. Now the boys and their father face a hard winter in a primitive dugout house. Looking for a better life, the father moves on farther westward, leaving the three brothers to care for one another. When at last the father sends for his sons, they must find their way out west alone, braving the dangers of the wilderness and fighting prejudice because of their skin color. 1–2.

Target Activity: "The Dangers of the Wilderness"

Define "wilderness" for the children. Ask if any of the children have hiked or camped in national parks or other places where wilderness still exists. Discuss the dangers of the wilderness that faces the three brothers in the story as they tried to find their way out west in the pioneer days. List the dangers on the board or overhead. Are these same dangers to be found in the wilderness today? What might be some different dangers that people might find today if they were trying to find their way in the wilderness?

Grades K–3

67 Lyon, George Ella (1993). *Dreamplace.* Illustrated by Peter Catalanotto. New York: Orchard.

Environmental Focus: Imagining what the environment was like for the Anasazi people

A park ranger leads a group up a path to the ruins of an Anasazi village, and a nameless narrator imagines what the environment and life were like for the native people who lived there in early times. As the narrator thinks of the environment and the details in the lives of the people, she imagines that the Anasazi people reappear and show their lives as they work and play, laugh and create, and then sadly, die, and leave nothing but their homes for posterity to find. K–3.

Target Activity: "An Anasazi Village and Its Environment as a Dreamplace"

Review the illustrations with the children and ask them to imagine that they have traveled to the environment of America's Southwest. Once there, ask them to imagine that they have looked up to the sky and seen an eagle soaring. Ask them to describe the eagle and other scenes such as the smells of the land and the hot dry air in the village, and the "castle-like" towers and courtyards of the village. Engage children in reflecting on some of the possible early life experiences of the native people for a dictation/writing experience, for a language experience chart, or for their journals.

68 Parrish, Peggy (1989). *Good Hunting Blue Sky.* Illustrated by James Watts. New York: Harper & Row.

Environmental Focus: Recognizing the link with nature that supported the survival of Native Americans

Blue Sky is going hunting for the first time in his young life. He tells his father, "Today I will bring home the meat." He shoots an arrow at the turkey and the turkey flees. He shoots at a deer and it, too, flees. Blue Sky decides to go after bigger quarry. When he sees a bear, he realizes it is too big, and Blue Sky climbs a tree. Feeling he has failed, Blue Sky starts toward home when suddenly he is attacked by a ferocious wild boar. Thinking quickly, Blue Sky leaps onto the boar's back and rides it all the way home, where his father shoots the boar with his bow and arrow. All the people in the village are invited to the feast, and Blue Sky tells them about the hunt. They change the young boy's name to Big Hunter. His feeling of autonomy is reinforced when he receives his new name from the villagers. K–3.

Target Activity: "Blue Sky's Environment"

Historical Fiction

Explain to children that in the history of the original Native American culture, young boys sometimes had to go out into their environment and bring home an animal to prove they were growing up. Relatedly, have children brainstorm some things that they would see in Blue Sky's environment if they had lived with Blue Sky and had gone along. Have them draw a picture of themselves with Blue Sky in the environment that they imagine and then show their drawings to the rest of the class.

Optional Activity: "Hunting: For Food or Pleasure?"

Discuss with children Blue Sky's reasons for hunting. Explain how early pioneers, as well as Native Americans, obtained most of their food through hunting. Ask children if they think this is a good purpose for hunting. Lead a discussion to help children clarify their feelings about the following situations:

- Deer hunting today when the deer is eaten;
- Deer hunting today just for sport; and
- Deer hunting today to affect the overpopulation of deer.

69 Rylant, Cynthia (1984). *When I Was Young in the Mountains.* Illustrated by Diane Goode. New York: Dutton.

Environmental Focus: Appreciating the link with nature that supports fond childhood memories

This excellent piece of historical fiction relates the memories of a girl's happy years growing up in the mountains of Virginia. She recalls her grandmother's kisses, her cornbread, and going to the swimming hole. The young girl's relationship with caring "others" is shown in the text and the pictures. She remembers visiting a country store and family evenings on the porch listening to frogs singing at dusk. 3.

Target Activity: "Stories of Earlier Days in Rural Areas"

Invite students to question an older friend or relative about early life experiences in a rural environment. Turn the experiences into a brief story with the title "When I Was Young," paying particular attention to how the person felt about his environment. After the stories are drafted, the students can team up with partners and read their stories to one another. While listening to the feedback from their partners, students use a colored pencil to write down the comments and suggestions on the draft. In a rewriting, students may choose to use or disregard these suggestions. The stories may be illustrated, their pages may be stapled together, and covers designed for display in the classroom book corner.

Grades K–3

70 Shub, Elizabeth (1982). *The White Stallion.* Illustrated by Rachel Isadora. New York: Greenwillow.

Environmental Focus: Appreciating creatures of nature that befriend humans

Little Gretchen is carried away from her wagon train by Anna, the old mare, to which her parents have strapped her. She is befriended by a wild white stallion who gently bites off the straps and sets her down. Scared and hungry, Gretchen cries herself to sleep. The next morning she drinks from a nearby stream and nibbles on grass. Remembering that her mother has told her to always stay where you are if you are lost, the child sits down to wait. The white stallion returns and tells Anna to return her to the wagon train — or so Gretchen believes. Gretchen survives her wilderness experience by not panicking, using her common sense, and remembering what her parents have told her, with the help of the white stallion. K–3.

Target Activity: "Surviving in a Frontier Environment"

Ask children to imagine that they are lost in a wilderness environment with nothing to eat or drink. Encourage them to consider what Gretchen did to survive. Discuss her actions. Ask the children to offer other suggestions as to what she might have done. To augment the discussion, ask children what three items they might bring on a hike to be "safe" in case they were to get lost.

71 Wetterer, Margaret K. (1990). *Kate Shelley and the Midnight Express.* Illustrated by Karen Ritz. Minneapolis: Carolrhoda.

Environmental Focus: Facing nature's fury during a storm

In this true story from the history of the 1880s. Kate Shelley, a young girl, shows her courage when she saves the lives of hundreds of people on a train racing toward a railroad bridge that, unknown to them, has been washed away during a dangerous storm. 1–3.

Target Activity: "A Powerful Storm in the Environment"

Invite the students to tell about some experiences during which they faced a powerful storm. Turn the experiences into an illustration with the title, "When I Was in a Powerful Storm." After the illustrations are completed, girls and boys may divide up into partnerships, show their illustrations to one another, and then discuss the event. After listening to the stories, children may assemble the illustrations into a book, design a cover and a table of contents, and place their book in the classroom reading/browsing corner.

Biographies

Stories from the biographical genre can lead children into unfamiliar worlds. A young child's appreciation and enjoyment of her environment in the Appalachian mountains, for example, is beautifully shown through the illustrations of Diane Goode in *When I Was Young in the Mountains*, a semi-autobiographical portrayal by Cynthia Rylant. This type of biographical fiction set in a particular period from history — a story of a person's appreciations, interests, and contributions — can encourage children to empathize with problems of the past and to compare them with the challenges faced by people in the present. For example, how might the child who appreciated growing up in the mountains in *When I Was Young in the Mountains* view living in the mountains as an adult today? A biography can help children to see another person's interests and experiences clearly and to realize that, while times change, the universal ongoing needs and concerns of people do not.

Additionally, authors of biographies for children have been quick to write about environmentalists, conservationists, and naturalists. Publishers have recognized the current interest in ecology by producing biographies (and fictionalized accounts) of "the greatest man and woman I never knew" — caring people who have made contributions in this area — and several of these books were selected for the following section.

72 Brandenburg, Aliki (1968). *A Weed Is a Flower.* Illustrated by the author. New York: Simon and Schuster.
   Environmental Focus: Appreciating the bounties of nature
   This biography of George Washington Carver gives information about his birth, early childhood and adult life. His story tells of slavery and freedom and poverty and success. Working as an agriculturalist chemist, Carver convinces farmers to grow peanuts as a crop and, in his laboratory, he makes approximately 300 products (such as soap and ink) from peanuts. Additionally, he gains recognition as a painter and is elected a Fellow in the Royal Society of

Arts in London, an honor given to few Americans. Born of slave parents, Carver earned his way through school and graduated from Iowa State College of Agriculture and Mechanical Arts. He joined the staff at Tuskegee Normal and Industrial Institute in Alabama and contributed his life savings to the George Washington Carver Foundation for Agricultural Research, a museum of his discoveries. Today, the George Washington Carver National Monument is on 210 acres of the farm where he was born. 3.

Target Activity: "Discoveries and Inventions"

Engage children in talking about discoveries and inventions that they wish were available, i.e., what is needed in their lives or in the lives of others? What are some of the steps that would be needed to complete the suggested discovery/invention? Who is interested in making cardboard/paper models of proposed inventions to show to others in the class? Who are the students who want to join together and initiate an "Inventors' Gang" to meet weekly after school to work on their proposed inventions? Who will contact a local business to support the needs (resources) of the Inventors' Gang? At a meeting, discuss the idea of patents and what a person would do to apply for a patent for an invention/discovery. A patent is a document protecting the inventor by giving him control of the manufacture and use of the invention for a certain number of years. For those interested in letter writing, information for securing a patent can be obtained from the Commissioner of Patents, Washington, D.C.

Additionally, review some of the contributions of Carver in agriculture, ideas which may turn the students' attention to the use of other plants. Carver explored the uses of the peanut plant for eating, for seed, and for animal feed which led to such products as salad oil, cosmetics, glycerin, insulation, paper board, feed meal, food flour, and fertilizer.

73 Norman, Gertrude (1960). *Johnny Appleseed*. Illustrated by James Carraway. New York: Putnam's.

Environmental Focus: Appreciating an early environmental hero

With a setting in the wilderness of colonial America, this is the story of the pioneer John Chapman (1774–1847), familiarly known as "Johnny Appleseed." It relates events from his childhood as a boy of seven years old, his experiences as Johnny Appleseed (given this name because he devoted his life to planting apple trees) and on to his days as an elderly man. Pioneer, apple lover, missionary — all describe Johnny "Appleseed" Chapman and his positive vision of life. 1–2.

Target Activity: "Describing Environmental Actions of Johnny Appleseed"

Biographies

Invite children to think of a picture of the actions of Johnny Appleseed as the teacher reads this description:

> Wearing a coffee sack for a shirt and a saucepan for a hat, Johnny Appleseed arrived in Ohio. He carried two things — a Bible and apple seeds. He was a friend to both white settlers and to Indians, to animals and the birds.

Invite the children to interpret the words about Appleseed being a friend to animals and birds and to create their own original illustrations of this pioneer's behavior. After the illustrations are finished, discussed and displayed, show the children the ways that Carraway and other artists have imagined the actions of Johnny Appleseed in their books.

Further, ask children to think of someone they know who could be called a modern-day Johnny Appleseed (male or female) and assign a new name such as "Mrs. Acorn." Discuss the way the person does his or her part to help the environment, e.g., by planting acorns for future oak trees, collecting acorns to give away, giving talks on the importance of planting oak trees, guiding people on parkway tours to point out plants and trees, or starting a campaign called "This Is the Year of the Oak." Ask children if they are interested in being a modern day "Johnny Appleseed" and have them identify a tree, plant, vegetable, or flower with which they want to identify. Engage them in selecting a nickname related to the identified flora and in meeting as a group to brainstorm ways they can take part in helping the environment. Back in the whole group, ask children to announce their "environmental names" and list them on an overhead transparency or a classroom chart. At selected times through the week, ask children to report on things they have done to help the environment.

Information

Informational books about the environment — nonfiction — can also be a valuable part of a child's reading menu. Informational books are readily available for young children and are becoming more and more popular; in fact, in the last few years publishers' lists have included as many informational book titles as fictional titles. Several of these books are sterling contributions. Some give an explanation of an aspect of the environment to help children appreciate and understand what is going on in ecology; a definitive biography of a naturalist, conservationist, or environmentalist; a presentation of the author's attitude toward a subject; an exploration of a topic that is undergoing change. The sample titles that follow will enable readers to pursue the reading and presentation of nonfiction about the environment successfully.

74 Albert, Burton (1993). *Windsongs and Rainbows.* Illustrated by Susan Stillman. New York: Simon & Schuster.

Environmental Focus: Observing the physical environment

Every component of the physical environment of a young child is observed in Burton Albert's lyrical evocation of the senses. The author invites children to see, hear, and feel the wind, the sun, the storm — and the calm that follows. Stillman's colorful paintings help bring all of nature alive in this celebration of our earth. K–2.

Target Activity: "Take Note of the Environment"

Provide children with a survey chart that includes the three senses mentioned in the book and label three columns "see," "hear," and "feel." In a walk around the school grounds, have children observe what they see, hear, and feel in their environment and write, or pictorially depict, their answers. When they return to class, discuss what each child noticed in his or her physical environment.

Information

75 Amsel, Sherri (1992). *A Wetland Walk.* Illustrated by the author. Brookfield, CT: Milbrook.

Environmental Focus: Endangered environments

Besides offering food and homes for a variety of plants and animals, wetlands stabilize the water table and filter sewage and other pollutants from water. Therefore, wetlands, with their fragile food chain, are not only important to the survival of wildlife, but to humans as well. *A Wetland Walk*, with delightful full-page watercolor illustrations and rhyming text, provides a close-up look at the numerous plants and animals that make the wetlands their home. That home, however, is an environment that is severely threatened by human activities. 2–3.

Target Activity: "What's in the Wetlands?"

Play a tape recording of natural sounds from the wetlands. Such tapes are available commercially in record and nature stores. Invite students to share what they imagined, supported by the illustrations in *A Wet Walk*. Compile a list of their suggestions.

With their list as a point of reference, help the children determine which plants and animals are most likely to be found in a wetland area. If possible, have them classify the plants and animals according to the kind of wetland in which they would be found. State or federal wildlife officials and representatives of private conservation or nature-related organizations can be helpful. "Wading into Wetlands" from the National Wildlife Foundation's Naturescope series includes much useful information on this topic as well.

76 Bang, Molly (1980). *The Grey Lady and the Strawberry Snatcher.* Illustrated by the author. New York: Four Winds.

Environmental Focus: Appreciating the importance of nature for food and protection

In this wordless story, the Grey Lady is all grey except for her face and hands and the strawberries she carries. She is stalked by a thief in a lime-green cape as she walks down the sidewalk and into a swamp. After several unsuccessful attempts to steal the berries, the thief tracks the lady into the grey background and trees of the swamp and discovers a bush of blackberries. Distracted while eating the berries, the thief doesn't see the Grey Lady arriving safely in her home where she gives the fruit to her family, the elderly, the children, and the baby. 1–3.

Target Activity: "Reading a Wordless Book about Nature's Food"

With children, review the illustrations on an opaque projector to identify ways that nature provides food and protection for humans. Write the children's suggestions on the board. Ask the children to relate the story to their everyday lives and suggest ways that nature provides food and protection for their families.

Optional Activity: "Food from Nature"

As an assignment after sharing this book with children, ask them to go home and make a list of everything that they have for dinner on a particular evening, with help, if necessary, from a parent or older sibling.

Back in the classroom, have children work in small groups to analyze where their food came from. Every food item should be traced back to an item in nature — either a plant or an animal. Every food item should then be examined in order to create a flow diagram which shows the major source of each food item — from the product the children eat to its origin from a plant or animal source. For example:

$$me \rightarrow milk \rightarrow cow \rightarrow grass$$

Some flow diagrams will be "short" ones; others will be long. Sometimes the children will not be sure what particular animals eat for food so they will want to ask a resource person or consult some library resources to find out.

77 Bare, Colleen Stanley (1993). *Never Grab a Deer by the Ear.* New York: Cobblehill.

Environmental Focus: Fostering an awareness of essential components of habitat

Colleen Stanley Bare uses beautiful color photographs to show young readers the difference between two kinds of deer that are native to North America, the white-tailed deer and the mule deer. She carefully describes the physical characteristics of each of these animals in words and through the photographs. The major purpose of the book is to explain to readers that in some areas of North America there are too many deer because humankind has destroyed their natural predators, whereas in other areas, there are too few deer because humans have destroyed the deer's habitat. 2–3.

Target Activity: "What Do Deer Need?"

After reading the book with children, discuss the point made by the author that all deer need good habitats in order to survive. Ask children to name the essential components of habitats as you write them on the board:

food   shelter
water   space in a suitable environment

Have children count off by twos. Have all the "ones" be white-tailed deer and all the "twos" be mule deer. Each of the deer will have factors that challenge their ability to maintain their populations over time, but the white-tailed deer will be threatened by humankind and the mule deer will be faced with natural disasters. Have small groups of white-tailed deer and small groups of mule deer each create one problem for themselves, for example:

Threats from Humans (White-Tailed Deer)
- Too much hunting
- Pollution
- Habitat destruction
- Building of highways and growth of recreational areas, cities and related services

Threats from Nature (Mule Deer)
- Early freezing
- Drought
- Disease
- Flooding
- Heavy snow

78 Baylor, Byrd (1978). *The Way to Start a Day.* Illustrated by Peter Parnall. New York: Scribner's Sons.

Environmental Focus: Getting acquainted with the significance of Native American tales about the stars

This Caldecott Award book portrays customs and traditions (and religious significance) related to the ways people from around the world greet the sun at the beginning of each day. Songs of praise or gifts to the sun take place in countries such as China, the Congo, Egypt, Japan, Mexico, Peru, and in the United States in Arizona and New Mexico. 1–3.

Target Activity: "A Special Time"

The author, Byrd Baylor, points out that greeting the sun is a universal custom and encourages the reader to think of a way to have his or her own special time with the sunrise to make the daily cycle of the sun more meaningful to the reader. Invite children further interested in this topic to meet in partners and discuss a way to have a special time at sunrise that would make the importance of the sun more meaningful to the child. Engage the children in sketching their ideas in illustrations to show their partners.

79 Baylor, Byrd (1978). *Everybody Needs a Rock.* Illustrated by Peter Parnall. New York: Scribner's Sons.

Environmental Focus: Becoming aware of the variety of rocks

This is an informational text about locating rocks and appreciating their composition. It is written simplistically and interestingly enough to appeal to very young children. K–3.

Target Activity: "Rocknasium"

Have each child find a rock and bring it with them into the classroom. Ask children to imagine that they are small enough to consider their rocks as mountains to climb. Ask them to image what it would be like to climb such a mountain. Invite comments about:

    1. the way they feel (small as an insect on a survival climb);

    2. the way they imagine the height of the rock-mountain's "walls" (imagine it soaring up as high as 25 feet with small rock projections)

80 Berger, Melvin (1992). *Look Out for Sea Turtles!* Illustrated by Megan Lloyd. New York: HarperCollins.

Environmental Focus: Fostering an appreciation of wildlife

Children will enjoy this informative book illustrated with soft watercolor pictures as they gain a deeper appreciation of the contribution of turtles to our lives. Showing various species of turtles in their environment, the author explains that the turtle's survival is dependent upon its protective shell and its willingness to eat a wide variety of food. Included is information about the turtle's life cycle as well as illustrations of 15 different species of turtles. 2–3.

Target Activity: "Turtle Research"

Have children select one of the 15 species of turtles described in this book to research. With the help of the librarian or resource person, have each child find three new facts about their chosen turtle by consulting the encyclopedia or other trade books. For children who are especially interested in sea turtles, have them request information by writing a letter to the following address:

    The Center for Marine Conservation
    1725 De Sales Street NW
    Washington, DC 20036

The Center will send free fact sheets about sea turtles as well as a sea turtle coloring book when interested students enclose $1.00.

81 Cameron, Elizabeth (1984). *A Wildflower Alphabet.* Illustrated by the author. New York: Morrow.

Environmental Focus: Appreciating the beauty of wild flowers in England and Scotland

Information

In a unique and originally composed book, beautiful full-color watercolors introduce children to the beauty of such flowers in England and Scotland's environment as the Willow Herb, Yellow Iris, Zenry, and others, and to related letters of the alphabet. The facts related to the flower descriptions and folklore are hand-lettered. The author's verses about the flowers are included. 1–3.

Target Activity: "Recognizing the Value of Flowers in Our Lives"

Introduce *A Wildflower Alphabet* (Morrow, 1984) by Elizabeth Cameron as a writing model and a way to collect further information about the value of flowers in our environment. With Cameron's book, the following links to writing and the environment can be demonstrated and discussed with the children:

1. an original composition is created by a grandmother for her grandchildren;
2. a wildflower can introduce each letter of the alphabet;
3. information about wildflowers can be hand-lettered;
4. a wildflower's beauty can motivate an author to write poetic verses;
5. a wildflower can motivate fanciful thought, e.g., "that the flowers will talk to you";
6. a person can "say it with flowers" and send a message to someone special with nature's beauty; additionally, the children may listen to and write about some of the "messages" that people have associated with flowers over time;
7. popular flowers such as roses, cowslips, pansies, and daisies have motivated poets to write lots of poems, but there is a lack of verses about the "unpopular" flowers and flowering herbs and vegetables (such as broccoli).

82 Carle, Eric (1993). *The Very Hungry Caterpillar.* Illustrated by the author. New York: Clarion.

Environmental Focus: Getting acquainted with the life cycle of a caterpillar

In this book, a child discovers the vocabulary for numbers, days and foods as he or she watches the hungry caterpillar eat its way through an increasing number of foods on the different days of the week until it turns into a beautiful butterfly. Pre–2.

Target Activity: "Introduction to Environmental Reader's Theater"

Ask volunteers to act as the narrator for a reader's theater production of this environmental life cycle, and if interested, children can send for a brochure

Grades K–3

about the reader's theater script of *The Very Hungry Caterpillar*. It arrives with games and vocabulary introduction for Carle's book from Readers Theatre Script Service, P.O. Box 178333. San Diego, CA 92177.

83 Carlson, Laurie (1993). *Ecoart: Earth-Friendly Art & Craft Experiences for 3-9 Year Olds*. Illustrated by Loretta Trezzo Braren. New York: Kids Can! Bks/Williamson.
   Environmental Focus: Collecting natural objects for art and craft projects
   Carlson's book presents ideas for collecting natural objects such as bark, twigs, pebbles, plants, and weeds to use as materials, and includes constructing bird feeders, making nature prints, recycling and composting activities. Step-by-step directions and the predicted amount of time to complete the projects are given. Pre–3.
   Target Activity: "Art and Ecology"
   With children, take a nature walk through the nearby area and ask them to collect some natural objects they see along the way — leaves, pebbles, twigs, and so on. Returning to the classroom, ask children to meet in pairs and identify what they found by labeling the objects with small cards made from index cards. Invite them to make nature collages by pasting the objects into pleasing arrangements on art paper. Display in the room.
   On a second trip, with lawn bags and a small shovel, take an ecology walk to the same area and ask children to collect objects that represent pollution they see along the way — mainly paper items thrown on the walk and in the gutter. Use the material to make pollution collages when back in the classroom.

84 Clements, Andrew (1992). *Mother Earth's Counting Book*. Illustrated by Lonni Sue Johnson. Saxonville, MA: Picture Book Studio.
   Environmental Focus: Taking environmental action
   The title of this book is misleading, for it is much more than a counting book and is appropriate for readers of many ages. It opens with, "One Earth ... just one" and progresses to the continents, seas, and poles, and along the way, inspires a new love and appreciation for the planet. The bright watercolor illustrations add richness to the text by providing unique views of Earth's important features. K–3.

Information

Target Activity: "Environmental Boxes"

Contact another teacher or librarian in another part of the state, the nation, or the world and arrange to exchange environmental boxes. The box can include a class photo, drawings, a mural, photos of the local environment, stories, poems, and natural objects from the school yard and local community (these can be gathered on a class walk or field trip). Choose students' work that is most representative of the local environment, and that which will help the other class of students to learn about your local environment and compare it with their own.

When your class receives an environmental exchange box from the other class, make a bulletin board to display the materials. Discuss the similarities and differences between your school and neighborhood environments and those of the other class.

85 Ehlert, Lois (1989). *Planting a Rainbow.* New York: Harcourt.

Environmental Focus: Learning about vegetables

Bold print combines with colorful illustrations to show how to plant vegetables that will grow into the ingredients for Daddy's soup. Also note Jeanne Modessitt and Robin Spowart's *Vegetable Soup*. Both are recommended to help young children see the connection between the food on their table and what grows in nature. K–3.

Target Activity: "Growing a Vegetable Garden"

From a local nursery obtain a small shatterproof greenhouse with a removable tray for cleaning. Also purchase some peat pellets and several packets of vegetable seeds. With the children, plant the seeds and discuss the other factors that will help the seeds grow into edible vegetables. When the plants have matured, harvest them and use them for a vegetable soup that the entire class can savor. Obtain recipes from the parents of children in the class.

86 Follett, Dwight W. (1961). *Little Creek Big River.* Illustrated by Robert Hodgell. Chicago: Follett.

Environmental Focus: Acquiring knowledge about water's journey from stream to sea

This Follett Read-to-Know book contains information to help children understand how a stream is formed and grows into a creek and then a river; how animals use it; how humans use it and control it; and how the river changes the land as it makes its way to the sea. The water cycle is also explained in simple terms, supported by the colorful illustrations. Rain falls. It flows into the river from seepage into the ground and from runoff. The river moves toward the ocean. Water evaporates into the air from the ocean, rivers, creeks, and streams. Winds carry the moist air far over the land where it appears as clouds in the sky. It then falls from the clouds as rain, completing the water cycle. 2–3.

Target Activity: "The River"

On the writing board or an overhead transparency, write down four columns with the following headings and list the understandings developed by the book under the appropriate headings:

Humans Use the River	*Animals Use the River*
As a highway	Fish live in it
For recreation	Animals build homes in it
For water supply	Animals get water
For sewage disposal	Animals get food
For water power	
For route through mountains	

Humans Change the River	*River Changes the Land*
With bridges	valleys
With tunnels	canyons
With levees	rapids and falls
With dams	sand bars
With locks	islands
	deltas

87 Gackenbach, Dick (1992). *Mighty Tree.* Illustrated by the author. New York: Harcourt Brace Jovanovich.

Environmental Focus: Becoming aware of endangered plants as well as the value of forests

The whole concept of forests and their importance in our lives is addressed here in a simple text with colorful illustrations that would appeal to primary age youngsters. Animals are not the only living things in danger of extinction — plants are too. Children see the power of tiny seeds in this book and also the possibility of destruction after many years of growth into "mighty" trees. The reader experiences the life of three trees from their "births" as seeds blown down to earth by the wind to their deaths, as the first is cut and made into paper, the second becomes a Christmas tree, while the third remains in the forest to provide seeds for new trees and to provide homes for many animals. The watercolor pen-and-ink pictures dramatize the growth from seedling to tree. K–3.

Target Activity: "Our Friend, the Tree"

Help children make a list of all the positive things trees do for our environment. Add to their list the fact that trees absorb carbon dioxide, the main gas that causes the "greenhouse effect." Take a field trip to a local nursery to find out what species of trees grow naturally in your area; purchase three seeds for an appropriate tree. Find out about planting the seeds by sending away for a free pamphlet called "Planting Trees" to the following address (enclose a self-addressed envelope):

> The Pennsylvania Resources Council
> P. O. Box 88
> Media, PA 19063

Optional Activity: "A World Without Paper"

Ask children to take a few seconds to imagine what life would be like without paper. Have them write down three ways their lives would be changed. Ask them to share orally the ways that they thought about. Similarly, ask children to imagine a world without trees and have them write down three ways their lives would be different. Assuming both trees and paper are important to our lives, then, what statements would they make about cutting down trees? For further information about paper and how it is made, refer children to Lynn Perkins's *Let's Go to a Paper Mill* (Putnam's Sons, 1969) or to *The Amazing Paper Book* (Addison-Wesley, 1989) by Paulette Bourgeois.

88 Glaser, Linda (1992). *Wonderful Worms.* Illustrated by Loretta Krupinski. New York: Millbrook.

Environmental Focus: Appreciating worms

Through illustrations, a very brief text, and supplementary information, readers will learn about the amazing earthworm. Featuring full-color illustrations of a garden, both above and underground, and the creatures that inhabit it, the book has a simple, straightforward informational text. K–3.

Target Activity: "Worm Observations"

Send a small group of children out to collect worms in plastic jars. You need one worm for every two students. Caution the children not to harm the worms. On the board or written on a ditto master to be copied and given to each pair of children, have them observe the worms and answer these questions, pictorially for younger children and in written form for older ones:

- What do you find interesting about the worm?
- Do you see a mouth? Try to imagine how and what the worm eats;

Grades K–3

- How does the worm move? Does it ever get tired? What makes you think so?
- Is the worm the same color all over? Is it clean? What is attractive about it?
- Where does the worm live? Do worms live in your neighborhood all year round? Why wouldn't you see worms when the temperature is cold?

Discuss the answers to questions with the whole class. Be sure to release the worms back where they were found when you are through studying them!

89 Glimmerveen, Ulco (1989). *A Tale of Antarctica*. New York: Scholastic

Environmental Focus: Becoming aware of the effects of pollution

This sad story concerns the slow polluting of one of our last frontiers — Antarctica. It begins in the springtime when the temperature rises and the snow begins to melt. With the thaw, the litter becomes evident. Oil drums and garbage are strewn all along the beaches. A father penguin is horrified when he sees his family and companions becoming entangled in the debris. One day, while he is hunting for food, he is caught in the oil slicks on the water and cries for help. His family alerts a team of environmentalists. They treat father penguin with a mixture of powdered clay to absorb the oil. When winter comes, the oil tankers leave; the people concerned with the wildlife and the penguins themselves are left wondering if the habitat will ever return to its original state. K–3.

Target Activity: "A Packaged Picnic"

Many foods that we eat come packaged naturally (such as fruits) while others, like crackers, are overly packaged using non-recyclable or non-biodegradable materials such as the ones in which the penguin family became entangled. As an assignment, or during a class field trip, have children carefully look at and compare wrapped and unwrapped oranges. As a consumer concerned about the environment, which would they buy? Plan a picnic using only foods that are not excessively packaged. Discuss what becomes of excess packaging. How does it affect the wildlife?

90 Goudey, Alice (1959). *Houses from the Sea*. Illustrated by Adrienne Adams. New York: Scribner's Sons.

Environmental Focus: Recognizing and appreciating shells

Near the waves lapping on shore, a young sister and brother collect many shells that at one time held small creatures of the sea. The two children gather specimens of angel wings, moon shells, slipper shells, periwinkles and others for rainy day play. A reader learns to identify the shell shapes with the aid of illustrations that match the shell shapes to objects the shells resemble. For example, the shape of a scallop shell is matched to the shape of a fan, and the shape of the small keyhole limpet shell is matched to the shape of an unusual hat. K–2.

Target Activity: "A Sea Creature's Point of View"

Have the children imagine that they are small enough to be on eye-level with a small creature of the sea. Ask them to imagine what it would be like to be an angel wing, a moon shell, slipper shell and so on. Invite their comments about:

    1. the way they feel when they are small (like a snail) in the environment;

    2. the way they imagine the size of other objects around them; and

    3. the worries and concerns they would have about predators and pollution.

91 Granger, Judith (1982). *Amazing World of Dinosaurs.* Illustrated by Pamela Baldwin Ford. Mahwah, NJ: Troll Associates.

Environmental Focus: Recognizing the extinction process of some of Earth's creatures

What happened to the giant creatures that ruled the earth for nearly 200 million years? Why did they become extinct? This book describes the major dinosaurs living at that time, their habitat and their eating habits. It also explores the many theories about why they disappeared, explaining scientific terms such as adaptation, climate, and extinction. 2–3.

Target Activity: "What Happened to the Dinosaurs?"

After reading this book aloud to children, ask children to recall the prevalent theories about the dinosaurs' extinction. Write them up on the board or overhead transparency under the question, "What happened to the dinosaurs?" as follows:

    What Happened to the Dinosaurs?
    A dreadful disease killed them.
    Smaller animals ate their eggs.
    The climate changed and Earth was too cold and dry.
    Their swamps dried up.
    Their food source (plants) changed.

Ask children to consider all the different theories or ideas proposed in the book and then answer the question orally, beginning with the sentence stem, "I think the dinosaurs became extinct because _____." Graph children's responses.

92 Heller, Ruth (1983). *The Reason for a Flower.* Illustrated by the author. New York: Grosset and Dunlap.

Environmental Focus: Acquiring knowledge about nature's flowers

This fascinating book shows readers, through beautiful full-color illustrations, the essentials of botany in a way that is interesting and understandable even for primary age youngsters. The intricate relationships among seeds, flowers, weeds, pollen, and animals are explored using actual scientific terminology ("flowers are known as angiosperms") that becomes less threatening in this delightful context. 2–3.

Target Activity: "Living Things Table"

Invite children to explore their environments when they leave school and to collect examples of seeds, weeds, and flowers. Label three sections of a table for children to display their living things and have children place them in the appropriate sections. As children bring in their examples of living things, revisit the book and see if they can find more information about their item from the text.

Optional Activity: "Seed Walk"

Ask each child to bring a large old fuzzy sock from home and put it over one shoe. Wearing the sock this way, go on a walk through a grassy area or field—particularly one that is a rich source of seed-bearing plants. Back in the classroom, have each child take the sock off and look at it. What has happened? Removing the seeds and other particles from the socks, the children can examine what they have brought back from the walk. Discuss with the children the major kinds of things they seem to have—seeds, grass, twigs. Next, talk about the seeds in greater detail, noting the different sizes and shapes they have found—big, small, narrow and thin, round, and so forth.

As a follow-up activity, the children can plant their seeds in a shoe box filled with planting medium. Have children water and care for their shoe box seed gardens regularly and observe what grows.

93 Hirschi, Ron (1992). *Seya's Song.* Illustrated by Constance R. Bergum. Seattle, WA: Sasquatch Books.

Environmental Focus: Acquiring knowledge about the relationship of the S'Klallam people to the salmon

Information

Hirschi portrays the world of the S'Klallam tribe in the San Juan Islands and in northwestern Washington state through the view of Seya, the grandmother of a contemporary Native American girl, and the girl herself. Seya's stories about her people's language and culture emphasize the relationship of the tribe to the salmon, the salmon to the changing seasons, and the seasons to the cycles of life. Includes an annotated glossary and an afterword with added facts. 3 up.

Target Activity: "Some Relationships with Nature Are Universal"
With the children in grade three or older, discuss the concept of universal relationships that is portrayed in the book: When an elderly member of a family passes on the language and culture of the family, emphasizing the family's relationship to the food needed for life and the food's relationship to the changing seasons, and comparing the seasons to the cycles of a family's lifestyle, then a reader can look to these relationships and call them universal since all people pass along their language and culture, need food, and recognize the way food is dependent upon the changing seasons.

94 Holling, Clancy (1941). *Paddle-to-the-Sea.* Illustrated by the author. Boston: Houghton Mifflin.
Environmental Focus: Becoming aware of America's Great Lakes region
Paddle-to-the-Sea is a small, painted hand-carved Indian and canoe that is placed in the waters of Lake Nipigon by the carver, a young boy. It journeys through all of the Great Lakes until it reaches the sea. Its journey provides information about the environment as it travels through the Sea Locks, Lake Erie and over Niagara Falls. 1–3.
Target Activity: "Making Predictions about the Environment"
With children, review the full-color illustrations and search for the image of Paddle-to-the-Sea in every picture. Additionally, ask children to make predictions about possible pollution at the different sites that they see in the illustrations or hear about in the text, e.g., the iron-ore mines in Duluth, a working sawmill, and a journeying lake freighter carrying cargo.

95 Kennaway, Adrienne (1992). *Little Elephant's Walk.* Illustrated by the author. New York: HarperCollins.
Environmental Focus: Acquiring knowledge about nature's food chain
This book is perfect for introducing children to the food chain and discussing ecosystems. Little Elephant and his mother take a walk through the plains and forests of Africa. They encounter many different creatures and

observe some who live in harmony with each other and some who do not. Each new discovery encourages an observation of the exact environment in which each animal can be found. By the end of Little Elephant's walk, children will be able to discuss which animals live in the plains and which live in the forests of Africa, as well as which ones live in harmony. 1–3.

Target Activity: "The Forests and Plains of Africa"

Using six feet of butcher paper and tempera paint, allow children to create a mural of the plains and forests of Africa as presented in this book. First, write the word "plains" on the board and discuss this land form. Have children recall the animals of Africa that live on the plains. Then write the word "forests" on the board and discuss such an environment. List the animals that live in the African forests. Divide the class into two groups. Let one group paint the plains environment and animals while the other group paints the African forest environment and animals.

96 Koch, Michelle (1993). *World Water Watch.* Illustrated by the author. New York: Greenwillow.

Environmental Focus: Acquiring knowledge about the ocean's creatures

This book introduces six creatures — green sea turtles, penguins, polar bears, seals, sea otters and whales — that live in the world's oceans and on surrounding lands, and discusses why they have become endangered creatures. Problems related to ecology are described and ways to help the animals' survival are included. K–3.

Target Activity: "An Author's Concern about Ecology"

With children, discuss the point of view of this author who pleads with her readers to "Watch over the world, / Watch over the water." Ask children what they could do in this role. Discuss what meaning the author's other words have for the children when she says, "Care for the earth, / Care for the sea. / So all of our friends can stay." Invite children to illustrate their suggestions and display their drawings in the classroom.

Optional Activity: "Ecological Pollution"

Conduct a field trip to a local waterway and have resident authorities answer, "What kinds of pollution is affecting this body of water and the animals that live in it?" Have children then list in their field notebooks five things they can do — starting today — in their own lives to reduce the number of pollutants they add to the environment. Some examples might be:
- Use soap products that do not contain phosphates;
- Buy recycled paper rather than plastic packaging;
- Buy only organically-grown produce; and
- Conserve water.

Information

97 Kuhn, Dwight (1993). *My First Book of Nature: How Living Things Grow.* Illustrated by the author. New York: Scholastic.

Environmental Focus: Appreciating ways living things grow

This book has a table of contents that is useful to guide a reader to a topic of interest. Over 30 species of birds, fish, insects, mammals, and reptiles are reviewed and shown in full-color photographs. Point out that the informational material is arranged according to the amount of time a particular living creature needs to develop and grow to adult stage. Pre–2.

Target Activity: "Wild or Domestic?"

Ask children to bring pictures to class of as many animals as they can find in magazines or newspapers at home. Explain that animals are all living things that are not plants. Once children have assimilated a collection of animal pictures, help them to classify them, allowing them to work in small cooperative groups. Discuss with children about wild animals and domesticated ones before they begin classifying. Once children have put their animals into either wild or domesticated categories, provide poster board or construction paper and glue and ask children to make two collages — one of wildlife animals and the other of domesticated animals from their animal pictures. Make a classroom gallery of the products. If desired, have children write or dictate what they did that led to the completion of their products — collecting pictures, classifying, making decisions — and display the record of the process they went through with their collages.

98 Lavies, Bianca (1989). *Lily Pad Pond.* Illustrated by the author. New York: Puffin/Unicorn.

Environmental Focus: Reviewing life cycle of a bullfrog

A fat little tadpole who lives among waterlilies in a woodland pond is followed from his time as a tadpole through his adult days as a bullfrog. The simple story comes to life with striking color photographs taken by award-winning former National Geographic photographer Bianca Lavies. Lavies has truly captured the unique intricacy and beauty of the watery world of the lily pond and its many natural inhabitants. K–3

Target Activity: "The Life Cycle of a Frog"

Give children drawing paper and have them fold it in half. On one side, with help from the photographs in the text, have them draw a picture of a tadpole. On the other half, have them draw a picture of a frog. Discuss with children the differences in the stages of the life cycle of the frog. In which stage are they more like fish? What are some similarities and differences between young and adult humans and young and adult frogs?

Grades K–3

99 Leedy, Loreen (1993). *Tracks in the Sand.* Illustrated by the author. New York: Doubleday.
Environmental Focus: Examining life cycle of loggerhead sea turtles
This book portrays the events in the life cycle of the large loggerhead sea turtles from mating at sea to the female's journey to the shore to lay eggs, to the female's desertion of the eggs and her return trip to the sea. The text depicts the deserted eggs as the soon-to-be hatchlings develop, break out, and then move toward the beach to the water. Shows that the life cycle continues as another female journeys back to shore to lay her eggs. Included are further informational notes for adults. K–2.
Target Activity: "Facts about Sea Turtles"
Return to the book's drawings and review the sea turtle's life cycle. Show the children how you use other reference sources and children's books to locate some of the information missing from this book, i.e., the large size of sea turtles, the timing of the mating season for sea turtles, and the dangerous trip that young hatchlings take to escape predators and reach the ocean. As an example, show children the illustrations in the book *Loggerhead Turtle: Survivor from the Sea* (Putnam's, 1974) by Jack Denton Scott.

100 Lobel, Arnold (1984). *The Rose in My Garden.* Illustrated by Anita Lobel. New York: Greenwillow.
Environmental Focus: Recognizing life in a garden habitat
This beautifully illustrated book consists of an add-on free verse poem about the various creatures and horticultural items that are found in the author's garden. Starting with "This is the rose in my garden," the author invites the reader to a breath-taking garden with zinnias, hollyhocks, marigolds, pansies, and peonies, to name just a few. 2–3.
Target Activity: "Add-On Garden Poem"
After hearing this free-verse poem several times, children will be eager to chime in and try their hands at memorizing it. Challenge children to write their own free-verse poems after making a list of flowers they like and other creatures they know of that could live in their fantasy gardens. Encourage children to use Lobel's poem structure if they wish, adapting it in this manner: "This is the lilac in my garden. This is the ant that crawls on the lilac in my garden," and so forth. Allow children to illustrate their garden poems.

101 Locker, Thomas (1984). *Where the River Begins.* Illustrated by the author. New York: E. P. Dutton.
Environmental Focus: Appreciating a river as an important part of our lives

Information

Thomas Locker takes his young sons on a journey to answer the question "Where did the river begin?" because the river that flows gently past their house is an integral part of their lives. Their grandfather takes them to the stream that is the beginning of the river, they swim in the river, camp by its banks, and experience a storm that causes the river to overflow its banks during their journey. The young reader comes away from this book with an understanding and appreciation of the constancy and depth of the river. 2–3.

Target Activity: "The Source of a River"

Have children select a famous river, such as the Mississippi, the Nile, or the Rhine, and find where it begins and at what point it flows into the ocean. For interested children, encourage them to find out other facts about "their" river and information about how people's lives are affected by living on the banks, of, or near to, the river. What jobs do the rivers provide? How is farming affected? What special problems are caused by living near rivers? How do people try to keep their rivers clean?

102 MacDonald, Golden (1974). *The Little Island.* Illustrated by Leonard Weisgard. New York: Scholastic.

Environmental Focus: Appreciating the environment through our senses

To read this beautiful Caldecott-winning book and view each colorful illustration is to experience vicariously the ecology of a small Northwestern island. The poetic text describes the wind, the tides, the fish surrounding the island, the spiders, the gulls, the flowers, the seagulls that raise their babies on the island, the kingfishers who build their nests on it, and finally, a little black kitten who learns from the island "natives" how an island is part of the land. The book takes the reader through all four seasons on the island and notes the various changes that occur with each one. The text is a true celebration of our ability to appreciate the environment through our senses. K–3.

Target Activity: "Living on an Island"

Read the text again to the children, asking them to listen carefully and imagine they are going to live on the island for a week. What sounds, smells, and sights or feelings are they experiencing? When they have finished listening to the book, paying particular attention to their senses, have them turn to a neighbor and tell him or her what it was like living on the island.

103 McMillan, Bruce (1986). *Counting Wildflowers.* Illustrated by the author. New York: Lothrop, Lee & Shepard.

Environmental Focus: Appreciating beauty of wild flowers

This colorful concept book combines learning basic counting skills with

Grades K–3

an appreciation for the beauty of wildflowers. Children learn to count, name the colors, and recognize and name the common wild flowering plants. Rather than using exotic plants, the author has selected wildflowers that can be found in many locations: fields, wooded areas, backyards, as well as vacant lots and city sidewalks. Endnotes tell where and when flowers can be found. K–2.

Target Activity: "Finding Wildflowers"

From the 20 wildflowers identified in the text, have children keep a wildflower notebook and be on the lookout for such flowers in their own environment. As they find the flowers, help them to write down the names of the flowers and where they were found and then have them draw a picture of the flowers. Alternatively, show children how to press flowers so that samples can be kept in their wildflower notebooks.

104 McMillan, Bruce (1992). *Going on a Whale Watch.* Illustrated by the author. New York: Scholastic.

Environmental Focus: Acquiring knowledge about whales

This book shows two children on a boat cruising off the coast of Maine to look at whales. The photographs show whale behavior that includes a headstand, a flipper wave, and a tail breach. While enjoying the sights, the children imitate each behavior of the large creature. Glossary included. K–3.

Target Activity: "Looking Closely on a Whale Watch"

Review the illustrations with the children. Point out that all that is visible in each photograph is the part of the whale related to its behavior, while a smaller illustration shows a side view of the entire whale and the way it looks under the water. Ask children to close their eyes and imagine what the entire whale looks like. Then, have them discuss what they imagined with partners and make a drawing of what "their" entire whale looks like. If needed, review the visual glossary at the end of the book.

105 McTrusty, Ron (1975). *Dandelion Year.* Illustrated by the author. New York: Harvey House

Environmental Focus: Acquiring knowledge about the life cycle of a dandelion

In this wordless book, McTrusty shows a natural event in pictures — the life cycle of a dandelion. A young girl interacts with animals among the trees while line drawings of the flower's cycle are emphasized against rich brown backgrounds and green leaf shapes. Review the illustrations a second time with children to discuss the brightness/dullness of the sun and the artist-

Information

author's use of brown dots and crosshatching strokes to show the seasons changing quickly during the life cycle. K–3.

Target Activity: Display for "I-can-explain-nature's-events-out-loud"

Invite children to the display to explain what they learned about the life cycle of the dandelion to another child or into a tape recorder for other children to hear later. Consider adding any or all of the following to the display:

1. Ask children to imagine some of the ways that the dandelion could have gotten its name and tell the whole group their ideas. Share with the group that the original name for the flower came from France. It was called "dent de lion" which means "tooth of the lion." Place pictures of dandelions in the display and discuss which feature of the flower would have caused people to give it this name. Which parts of the flower do the children think resemble the lion's teeth? the toothlike flower petals? the toothlike edge of the flower's leaves?

2. The natural event of seasons shown in the prints and the pictures in *Ring of Earth: A Child's Book of Seasons* (Harcourt, Brace Jovanovich, 1986, 1–3) written by Jane Yolen and illustrated by John Wallner. Read aloud some of the metaphorical writing that tells of the nature of the world, and emphasize the symbol (and shape) of a ring in Yolen's book. Discuss the idea that the theme is seen in the book's title and that the ring represents the circle of seasons as well as the sound of nature heard in the weasels' song and the "songs" of the tiny pond frog, the dragonfly, and the flying goose.

3. Discuss the clear illustrations of the reproductive cycle of a moth in the circular story, *The Apple and the Moth* (Pantheon, 1970, Pre–1), by Iela and Enzo Mari. Ask the children to make predictions about what will happen when they see the silhouettes of the seasons' changes during the year. First in the sequence of details in this wordless book, an egg hatches into a worm and then the moth larva feeds inside the apple. When ready, it emerges from the apple and spins a cocoon. From the cocoon, the transformed moth flies off and lays its final egg on an apple blossom. This helps children develop their oral skills about sequencing, prediction, and evaluation.

106 Maestro, Betsy (1992). *Take a Look at Snakes.* Illustrated by Biulio Maestro. New York: Scholastic.

Environmental Focus: Appreciating wildlife

Though most children love animals, one exception to that rule is the often maligned snake. This book explores the physical appearance of snakes, their eating habits, and their defensive behaviors. The vivid pencil and watercolored illustrations show the characteristics and camouflaging abilities of

Grades K–3

many species of snakes. The author maintains that people are the most fearsome predator of snakes: each year thousands of harmless snakes are killed by people because they are erroneously considered to be poisonous or because their habitats have been destroyed. K–3.

Target Activity: "Camouflage for Survival"

Make a surprise terrarium for your students and bring it to class. The terrarium should contain a garter snake or another denizen of your area that uses camouflage as an adaptation technique. If children do not immediately find the snake who is living in the terrarium, have them look very closely until they do.

Ask children to think of other animals that blend in with their environment. Show photos or bring in magazines and ask children to look for pictures of animals that blend into their surroundings — they look like where they live so that they are hard to see. Explain that "camouflage" is one way animals adapt in order to survive.

Allow the children to participate in the process of returning the snake to its natural home in the wild. This is an excellent time to discuss human responsibilities for proper care of animals used for instructional purposes, as well as a potential way to see the snake camouflaged in a natural setting. An informative companion piece to this book is Maria Angel Julivert's *The Fascinating World of Snakes* (Barron's, 1993).

107 Manson, Christopher, adapter (1993). *The Tree in the Wood.* Illustrated by the adapter. New York: North-South Books.

Environmental Focus: Appreciating the contributions of trees

Manson's oversize picture book is adapted from a traditional folksong, "The Green Grass Grows All Around." The lyrics of *The Tree in the Wood* portray the life cycle of a tree beginning with the mature tree and ending with an acorn a boy has planted that has grown into a sapling. K–1.

Target Activity: "What Trees Give Us"

Read children another book about trees entitled *The Giving Tree* by Shel Silverstein, which poignantly tells of a young boy's relationship with a tree that gave and gave and asked for little in return. Brainstorm with children what their lives would be like without trees, then talk about all the things trees give us, and write the children's ideas on the board. Finally, introduce the idea of "giving back to the environment." Trees give us so much, so how can we take better care of them? Why could a tree be considered "your tomorrow?" List the ideas that the children have related to ways we can take good care of trees, such as:

- Let the bark of the tree grow naturally—don't carve initials in them;
- Water and fertilize trees;
- Leave the tree in a natural state—don't pull off limbs and leaves;
- Never cut trees down needlessly; and
- Always replace a tree that has been cut down.

108 Martin, Bill, Jr., and John Archambault (1988). *Listen to the Rain*. Illustrated by James Endicott. New York: Henry Holt.
Environmental Focus: Reviewing sounds and actions of rain

Using rhyme, rhythm and repetition, the authors use words and soft pictures to evoke the feelings and mysteries of the rain. They ask the reader to observe that rain can be loud and pelting and also be accompanied by crashing thunder, but that at other times it can be fresh, gentle, and almost a whisper, feeling very silent to the observer. Perfect to read before, on, or after a rainy day. K–2.

Target Activity: "Rain"

Have children brainstorm some words to describe hard, pelting, thunderous rain, as well as soft, gentle, dripping rain. Have each child choose words from the brainstorming to complete the following sentence: "Sometimes, rain is _____ but at other times, it seems _____.

Compile all the children's reflections into a class book about rain.

109 Miller, Edna (1971). *Duck, Duck*. Illustrated by the author. New York: Holiday House.
Environmental Focus: Reviewing the life of a mallard drake

This is the true story of the life of a mallard drake that could only have been written by a true nature lover. The author first encounters the drake as he is meeting his mate on a nearby pond. Life is easy and food is plentiful. One day, he goes back to the nest and finds that a fox has killed his mate. He is left to raise two ducklings that have just hatched. The ducklings grow up and head south for the winter, but the mallard stays behind, hoping his mate will return. Children give him bits of bread and he becomes very tame. He flies to a barn and begins to eat and sleep with the chickens who live there. One morning, hearing ducks above, the mallard heads back for the pond and finds a new mate. 2–3.

Target Activity: "Taking Care of Wild Pets"

Discuss with children why the mallard did not fly with the flock to a warmer climate. Was he really waiting for the return of his mate who had been killed by a fox? The author believes so. Ask the children what they think they should do if they find a wild bird (or animal) that has been separated from his or her flock (or group). Consult a forest or park ranger to compare viewpoints.

110 Mills, Patricia (1993) *Until the Cows Come Home.* Illustrated by author. New York: North-South Books.
Environmental Focus: Appreciating the beauty of rural life
This is a photographic essay with hand-colored photographs that shows scenes in the country. For each illustration there is a single line of text that describes such rural scenes as sunflower fields, bales of hay, and images of cows. K–2.
Target Activity: "Seeing the Beauty of Country Life"
Review the scenes with the children and invite them to contribute anecdotes from their real life experiences that are related to the scenes. Discuss some of the simple pleasures found in country life such as:
 1. rag rugs hanging out to dry and flapping on the clothes lines in the wind;
 2. a road-side self-service vegetable stand;
 3. bluebirds and coneflowers; and
 4. a biker, all alone, pedaling down a rural road.

111 Mizymura, Kazue (1971). *If I Built a Village.* Illustrated by the author. New York: Crowell.
Environmental Focus: Recognizing that people affect the environment
In this whimsical poetic text, the author shares with young readers what an ideal village might be. Her ink-and-wash drawings and joyous watercolor paintings show us an environment that can be naturally beautiful if it is cared for regularly. In Mizumara's village, owls hoot at night in the nearby forest, fish "flicker and swirl through streams," and birds "soar to the sky." But most important to the village are the people who "care and share with all living things, the land they love." 2–3.
Target Activity: "An Ideal Village"
Have children create an "ideal" village as author Mizymura did.
On the board, list the features of the environment:
- air
- animals
- plants

Information

- people
- space
- water

Have children brainstorm how each feature of the environment would be in their ideal village and write their responses next to the feature, e.g., for "space," there would be lots of land for each family; for plants, there would be many varieties of healthy trees, beautiful vegetable, herb, and flower gardens, and many parks.

Select five children to be in a group to "flesh out" more about each feature. Using a piece of butcher paper that covers an entire wall, allow the groups to portray their features using tempera paints, showing what their ideal, environmentally aware village would look like.

112 Myers, Christopher A., and Lynne Born Myers (1991). *McCrephy's Field.* Illustrated by Norman Chartier. Boston: Houghton Mifflin.

Environmental Focus: Acquiring knowledge about reclaiming nature's land

The beautiful finely-detailed watercolor illustrations in this simple story reveal how an abandoned field would be reclaimed by nature if humans left it to itself. Joe McCrephy used to farm the Ohio field in question and then left for Wyoming to raise goats with his brother. The reader is treated to the field as it returns to its natural state: wildflowers begin to grow, as do small trees; birds fill the trees; the red barn weathers and turns to "natural" gray. When Joe McCrephy returns, he hardly recognizes the overrun field, except for the remains of the barn. 1–3.

Target Activity: "Farmed or Fallow?"

Using both sides of a sheet of construction paper and crayons, have children draw pictures of the field as it was when Joe McCrephy was growing corn on it, and then as it became when it was abandoned to "fallow." Have children share their pictures in small groups and discuss the differences in the two fields. Ask them to respond to the following questions when sharing their pictures: what would happen to the birds if all fields were farmed? What would we eat if no fields were farmed? Where do the wildflowers come from?

113 Norris, Luanne, and Howard L. Smith, Jr. (1979). *An Oak Tree Dies and a Journey Begins.* Illustrated by Allen Davis. New York: Crown.

Environmental Focus: Reviewing the life and death cycle of an oak tree

With realistic pen-and-ink drawings, this book gives a scientific account of an oak tree. The oak grows on the bank of a river until the night it is uprooted in a storm. As the rains come in the spring, the tree moves into the river and becomes a log, then a piece of driftwood. Sometimes animals find shelter in it; other times mussels attach themselves to it. Finally, a boy finds the driftwood on the beach and is fascinated by its shape and color. He takes it home and puts it on a shelf in his bedroom, wondering sometimes where it came from and what has happened to it along the way. The text tells the reader how a tree, even after it dies, is still an important part of our environment. 2–3.

Target Activity: "The Journey of an Oak Tree"

Have children draw the oak tree as it was on the bank of the river, as a log floating in the river, and finally as a piece of driftwood adorning a boy's shelf. Invite the children to use their drawings to tell about each stage of the oak tree during its journey and how it is an important part of our environment in each stage.

114 O'Donnell, Elizabeth Lee (1991). *The Twelve Days of Summer.* Illustrated by Karen Lee Schmidt. New York: Morrow Junior Books.

Environmental Focus: Appreciating seasonal change from spring to summer

This is a perfect book to help young children begin to appreciate the beauty of their environment even as they are vigorously taking part in it. In a take-off of "The Twelve Days of Christmas," O'Donnell has each of the first twelve days of summer filled with sandpipers, seals, waves crashing, purple sea anemones, squid, flying fish, pelicans, dolphins, jellyfish, crabs and starfish. The cheerful illustrations support the sing-aloud text. K–3.

Target Activity: "Some Season Singalongs"

After reading and singing along with *The Twelve Days of Summer* several times, ask children to brainstorm some natural items they observe in their environment other times of the year, e.g., wintertime. Using O'Donnell's spirited format, help them to write a new song in celebration of a different season, e.g., "On the first day of winter I saw upon the lake, a multi-sided crystal snowflake."

115 Openheim, Joanne (1968). *Have You Seen Birds?* Illustrated by Barbara Reid. New York: Scholastic.

Environmental Focus: Acquiring knowledge about birds

This simple text, with three-dimensional clay illustrations, sorts birds

Information

into categories by actions (fishing birds), color (brightly breasted birds), habitat (sky birds, sea birds, marsh birds, field birds, farm birds, park birds, woodland birds) and other features:
1. by light conditions: night birds;
2. by physical characteristics: long-legged birds;
3. by seasons: autumn birds, early summer birds, and spring birds; and
4. by size: tiny "bug-sized" birds.

Related to the categories, the author asks the reader, "Have you seen birds?" In each category, while not identifying specific bird names, the author describes the actions of the different kind of birds in it. A refreshing way to think about birds. K–3

Target Activity: "A Bird Chart"

Using chart paper, make a category for each type of bird introduced in this text (some will overlap). Bring together some easy-to-read resources about birds and encourage children to find specific birds that would be appropriate for each category, e.g., sea birds: osprey, sea gull, frigate, pelican, sandpiper, etc. Invite children to illustrate each entry.

116 Pallotta, Jerry (1991). *The Underwater Alphabet Book.* Illustrated by Edgar Stewart. Watertown, MA: Charlesbridge Publishing.

Environmental Focus: Acquiring knowledge about life inhabiting a coral reef

Beginning with Angelfish and ending with the Zebra Pipefish, this book introduces different creatures that live among the coral reefs and shows them in full-color. The author briefly discusses a little bit about the life of each fish in the text. 1–3.

Target Activity: "Environmental Center with Alphabet Books"
Study the earth's waters with the following books:
- for children interested in the ocean:
Jerry Pallotta's *The Ocean Alphabet Book* (Charlesbridge, 1986, 1–3) introduces fish and other creatures that live in the North Atlantic Ocean. Isaac Asimov's *ABCs of the Ocean* (Walker, 1970, 2–3) features word blanks where a reader can collect and write a choice of words and definitions related to the ocean. A pronunciation guide is included for words that might be difficult, such as xiphosurous, phytoplankton, and ichthyologist. Keith A. McConnell's The *SeAlphabet Encyclopedia Coloring Book* (Stemmer House, 1982, 3 up) includes black and white sketches of sea life that are accompanied by informative paragraphs.

- for those interested in the habitat and life cycle of a fruit tree:
  Miska Miles's *Apricot ABC* (Little, Brown, 1969, K–3) tells the life cycle of the apricot from seed to tree in rhyming verses and shows the tree's habitat in accompanying illustrations.
- for children interested in a land-bound pond as a habitat:
  Judi Freedman's *ABC of a Summer Pond* (Johnny Reads, 1975, 2–3) illustrates life in and around a pond of such living creatures as a beaver, a silver bass, a crayfish, and others.
- for those interested in conservation and caring for the environment:
  Ivan Green's *Conservation from A to Z* (Oddo, 1968, 2–3) reviews conservation practices as well as the use of earth's natural resources from a conservationist's point of view and defines related conservation terms such as erosion and humus. Harry Milgrom's *ABC of Ecology* (Macmillan, 1972, 2–3) introduces ecology concepts that are accompanied by black-and-white photographs and informative text.

117 Parker, Nancy Winslow (1992). *Working Frog.* Illustrated by the author. New York: Greenwillow.

Environmental Focus: Understanding what an animal might feel like when it is captured

This winsome story follows a frog who has been captured and taken to a zoo. The frog tells the story of getting settled in his new environment and shares his feelings about starting a new life. This humorous picture book is arranged in four short chapters that provide lots of useful information about frogs, amphibians, and reptiles. The pen, watercolor, and colored pencil illustrations will help children see the different emotions that an animal might feel making an adjustment to becoming a "working" animal. K–3.

Target Activity: "A Day in Captivity"

Have children close their eyes and take them on an imaginary journey from a carefree Saturday afternoon playing with their friend to being captured and put in a cage by an unknown force. Lead them through a visualization where they must imagine staying in the cage waiting for meals while strange beings stare at them from the other side of the bars on the cage. How would they feel? Would they ever adjust? How do they feel this scenario compares with the dilemma faced by wild animals that are captured and placed in zoos?

Information

118 Roop, Peter, and Connie Roop (1992). *Our Earth, a Multitude of Creatures*. Illustrated by Valeris A. Kells. New York: Walker.

Environmental Focus: Acquiring knowledge about the connections among animals in their ecosystems

In this story, readers will gain an appreciation for the interdependence of animals within one of our world's many ecosystems. Set in the Pacific Northwest, the book shows indigenous animals involved in their activities over the course of an entire day. Exciting double-page illustrations show closeups of various animal groups. For example, readers are shown ravens attacking a hawk, a frog catching a fly as another frog jumps into the pond, and an owl catching a fly as other owls observe. The unusual names for each animal group are also presented. K–3.

Target Activity: "A Day in the Life of an Animal"

Ask children to select an animal from those presented in *One Earth, a Multitude of Creatures*. Using construction paper and pencils, encourage them to sketch their chosen creature across the span of an entire day, involved in its various activities of survival. Have children use their pictures to tell about their animal's activities sequentially.

119 Schlein, Miriam (1959). *When Will the World Be Mine?* Illustrated by Jean Charlot. New York: W. R. Scott.

Environmental Focus: Recognizing that nature and animals coexist

Though out of print, this book may be found in the children's section of a library's Caldecott Medal Award Collection. This is the story of a small snowshoe rabbit who finds out what it's going to be like to live in his environment. After his ears grow large enough to hear what's going on, the rabbit discovers that when he's thirsty he can drink from a nearby stream; when he's hungry, he can eat the grass and the bark of the trees; when he takes time to sniff with his nose, he can smell the scent of danger; and when he's in danger, he can hide in the thicket of plants. When winter comes, the rabbit has another survival feature: he has grown a coat of fur as white as the snow that falls, which means he can continue to live safely in his environment. Pre–1.

Target Activity: "How Did Nature Cooperate with the Snowshoe Rabbit?"

With children, discuss the needs of the rabbit and what nature provided. As the children recall certain facts, write the facts on a classroom chart or on the board:

Grades K–3

What the Rabbit Needed	*What Nature Provided*
1. water	1.
2. food	2.
3. shelter	3.
4. protection from danger	4.

Ask the children to fold a sheet of paper in half and select one of the things the rabbit needed as well as the corresponding way that nature provided for this need. Ask children to draw pictures that illustrate both ideas, with one idea on each side of the folded sheet. Take time to have the children show their illustrations and tell about them. Collect the drawings and place them in a group book entitled, "How Nature Cooperates with the Snowshoe Rabbit," or with another title the children suggest.

120 Schweninger, Ann (1993). *Springtime*. Illustrated by the author. New York: Viking.

Environmental Focus: Acquiring knowledge about spring

This book introduces the spring season and shows a dog family with human behaviors as they plant a garden, look closely at nature and go on a field day outing. A reader sees spring events such as the beginning of the baseball season, the blooming of flowers, and the arrival of returning birds. Explains how rain is created and how animals and plants grow. Gives directions for starting vegetable and flower seeds inside in egg cartons. K–2.

Target Activity: "Starting Seeds"

With children, review the directions for getting seeds to grow indoors by planting them in an egg carton. Give children some bean seeds and engage them in planting them indoors. Start a chart to record the daily observations of the growth of the seeds, when the seeds are watered, whether the day is sunny or cloudy, and other pertinent information.

121 Shelby, Anne (1993). *What to Do about Pollution* ... Illustrated by Irene Trivas. New York: Richard Jackson/Orchard.

Environmental Focus: Acquiring knowledge about the effects of pollution

This book introduces the problem of pollution as well as other social problems and asks such questions as, "What to do about pollution?" ("Stop it. / Clean it up.") and "What to do about the friendless?" and so on. Suggestions for the solutions are shown in the illustrations that portray multi-ethnic and intergenerational people. The book also shows people lined up at

Information

a soup kitchen, an old man said to be friendless, and several people who appear quite sad. K–1.

Target Activity: "Children Taking Environmental Action"

Ask the children to identify world problems as presented in the book as well as others that they know about. Some examples might be:

    hunger
    overpopulation
    poverty
    war
    waste

Have the children pick one of these topics, or one you are currently studying, and list all the possible solutions they can think of to help solve the problem. Identify appropriate government officials to whom the children may write to share their ideas. For children seeking more information specifically about pollution, send a self-addressed stamped envelope to the following address:

    Local Solutions to Global Pollutions
    2121 Bonar Street
    Berkeley, CA 94702

122 Sill, Cathryn (1992). *About Birds: A Guide for Children.* Illustrated by John Sill. New York: Peachtree.

Environmental Focus: Acquiring knowledge about the characteristics of birds

This book introduces the unique characteristics of the American robin, the Canadian goose, the Great Horned Owl, and other birds through illustrations showing related habitats and simple text. Additional facts are in the Afterword. Pre–2.

Target Activity: "A Nature Center"

Ask children to share times from their experience when they have visited a nature center, observed birds and land animals, or been in a nature area. Invite children interested further in Kenni, a screech owl, or the topic of a nature center to write for more information to Sue Wittorff, Director of Effie Yeaw Nature Center c/o Ancil Hoffman Park, Carmichael, CA 95608.

Optional Activity: "An Owl's Diet"

Locate some owl pellets (this is the undigested part of an animal that the owl "coughs" up) that can be found in a forest under trees or in abandoned buildings where owls may roost, or they may be purchased from scientific supply distributors.

Divide children into small groups. Give each group a pellet and ask children to try to separate the bones from the fur in their pellet using a pencil.

Try to determine if there are bones from more than one animal in the pellet. Lay out the bones in each pellet to form as complete a skeleton as possible. Skeletons may be glued onto a poster board for display. Discuss what the children have learned about the diets of owls by taking part in this activity.

123 Singer, Marilyn (1989). *Turtle in July.* Illustrated by Jerry Pinkney. New York: Macmillan.

Environmental Focus: Appreciating the seasons with unrhymed verses

All the seasons are celebrated in this book of poetry about animals in their natural environment. Every month a different animal is highlighted, using the unique perspective of that particular animal. Jerry Pinkney's luminous illustrations add to the sense of natural wonder offered in this lovely text. All ages.

Target Activity: "The Animal's Point of View"

Have children select a month of the year that they particularly like as well as an animal that they often see at that time of year. Using a variation of Singer's unrhymed verse, have children write a short verse about the month from their animal's point of view. Provide trade books, encyclopedias, and other resource materials to allow children to research the animal's habitat and diet, as well as the plants and flowers that would bloom in the month they have chosen.

124 Sis, Peter (1992). *An Ocean World.* New York: Greenwillow.

Environmental Focus: Appreciating ocean creatures

This is a unique animal story concerning freedom and captivity. Peter Sis's expressive pen, ink, and watercolor illustrations tell the story of a whale raised in captivity and then released back into the ocean. This humorless wordless book follows the whale's journey to find a friend and mate — a search made more difficult because she has never seen another whale. K–2.

Target Activity: "Adopt-a-Whale"

Show children a clip from the video *Free Willy* that also underscored the problems of whales raised in captivity. Ask children if they would be interested in "adopting" a whale. For more information on how to do this, write:

Pacific Whale Foundation
Kealia Beach Plaza
101 N. Kihei Road
Kihei, Maui, HI 96753-8833

Information

125 Tresselt, Alvin (1946). *Rain Drop Splash.* Illustrated by Leonard Weisgard. New York: Lothrop, Lee & Shepard.
Environmental Focus: Recognizing the continuity of nature
This book follows the path of a rain drop as it travels from a pond to a brook, then to a lake and a river and finally out to sea, just as *Paddle-to-the-Sea* did in Hollings' informational book. K–2.
Target Activity: "The Journey of a Rain Drop Today"
Mention the time period in which the book was published and the simple way that the author and artist told about the travels of the rain drop, and then ask the children what a rain drop of today might see if rain fell in their area. Let the children dictate their ideas and write the ideas on the board or on an overhead transparency. Ask the children to work with partners and bring this story up to date with their own drawings to show the way of life and society that a rain drop would see in its travels.

126 Udry, Janice May (1956). *A Tree Is Nice.* Illustrated by Marc Simont. New York: Random House.
Environmental Focus: Recognizing the value of trees
Trees are beautiful; they fill up the sky. You can roll in the leaves of a tree and climb up its trunk. This Caldecott winner tells these and other reasons why "a tree is nice." The book encourages youngsters to plant a tree so that they can watch it grow and many years later say to people, "I planted that tree!" K–3.
Target Activity: "Plant a Tree"
Have children dictate (or write, for older students) a letter to the Department of Agriculture asking for tree seeds which they will send, free of charge. Distribute copies of the dictated letters to each child. Allow each child to draw a picture on the bottom of the letter of what the tree will look like when it is fully grown. Discuss with children why it is important to save and restore our forests. When the seeds arrive, plant them in small paper cups. Once the seeds have sprouted, have the children donate them to the school and offer to plant, water and take care of them as a class project.

127 Wallwork, Amanda (1993). *No Dodos: A Counting Book of Endangered Animals.* New York: Scholastic.
Environmental Focus: Acquiring facts about endangered species
For a delightful overview of endangered species for younger readers, this

Grades K–3

book is a "must." The book is illustrated with dynamic, colorful collages on each page. The endnotes offer helpful information about the threats to the endangered animals listed. The simple picture story book is predictable, allowing young children to read it independently. The counting progresses from one to ten and culminates with a blank page — no picture and no dodos — to graphically illustrate the reality of extinction. K–2.

Target Activity: "Preventing Extinction"

Write the word "extinction" on the board or an overhead transparency and explain to children what the word means and that "extinction" is what happened to the dodo in the book.

Ask children to help you make a list of things people do that seem harmful to wild animals. Ask them to think of things they have seen or know about that might be harmful. Some of these could be:

- picking up baby animals in their environment (fawns, baby birds, etc.)
- driving cars or other vehicles over a fragile environment
- destroying birds' nests
- killing, collecting, harassing or owning wildlife
- seeing power company employees cut and trim limbs from trees that contain nests of squirrels, birds, etc.

Have children use cut-out photos or drawings to make these activities into cards describing what is happening (or teachers can prepare cards in advance). Collect the cards. Count children off into groups of four. Hand out one card to each group and ask them to present a short skit to the class to show what is happening or have them discuss the following points:

- What is happening?
- Does it harm wildlife? How?
- Is it good or bad behavior? Why?
- Is the person doing it having fun? Doing it as part of a job?

After the groups have shared their ideas about their cards, ask them to think of alternative actions that people could take that would not be harmful to wild animals or their habitat.

128 Waters, Sarah (1992). *Hidden Animals.* Illustrated by Teresa O'Brien. New York: Morris.

Environmental Focus: Acquiring facts about nature's creatures

This book from the Secrets of Nature series offers thick pages that small hands can turn, and good-sized tabs to push and pull, making these simple descriptions of animal behavior interactive and fun. In "Growing Up," readers

Information

see eggs hatch into birds and baby salmon grow up in a stream before moving out to an ocean habitat. How animals camouflage themselves is revealed in the book as a reef opens up to show a moray eel and striped clown fish, and in the Arctic, a hare turns from white to brown when the season changes. K–3.

Target Activity: "Hiding in Nature"

Take children out to a wooded area, blindfold one student who will be the "predator." The predator counts to 20 slowly while the other children hide. The predator must then take off the blindfold and see how many "prey" he or she can find without moving, identifying who they are and describing where they are. If found, these "prey" have been "eaten" and now become predators in the game. When only one or two children are left hidden, have them stand up and identify themselves. It may be surprising to the "predators" how close some of the "prey" actually were to them — an example of successful adaptation because of how well they blended in with their environment in order to survive. Explain the term "adaptation" in relation to the game and the information in the book *Hidden Animals*.

129 World Wildlife Fund (1988). *All About Pandas.* San Francisco: Determined Productions, Inc.

Environmental Focus: Keeping animal resources safe

This tiny book about the giant panda is one of a World Wildlife Series that also includes *All About Tigers, All About Koalas,* and *All About Snow Leopards.* Besides explaining why many people worldwide love pandas, the book also explains that there are fewer than 1000 pandas left living in the wild and urges the reader to do everything he or she can to keep giant pandas safe in their forest homes. K–2.

Target Activity: "Protecting Wild Animals"

Ask children to brainstorm some things they think they could do to help animals that are in danger of becoming extinct. Explain that there is an agency already set up for the protection of all wild animals. It is called the World Wildlife Fund. Suggest that the class think of ways they could raise money for the fund, e.g., by collecting discarded papers, aluminum cans, or selling lemonade. Then encourage children to join and send their contributions to:

World Wildlife Fund
Membership Department WP88
1250 24th Street, N. W.
Washington, DC 20037

Grades K–3

130 Yolen, Jane (1976). *Milkweed Days.* Illustrated by Gabriel Amadeus Cooney. New York: Crowell.

Environmental Focus: Appreciating summer flowers seen in the country

In late summer, the milkweed flowers come out along with the Queen Anne's Lace, King Devil, Bluets, Rye and sweet-smelling Clover. Any child growing up in the country, like the three children in this book, learns to interact with nature. They know the secret of the milkweed pod: it will burst open and fly away so the children can run and catch the "silky birds." Cooney's photographs are evocative of the sights, smells, and sounds of a summer day in the country. K–3.

Target Activity: "Nature Walk"

Heighten children's awareness of the beauty of nature around them by taking a walk to the nearest park or nature reserve in your area. Have them keep a survey chart of all that they see, hear, and smell in nature. Invite them to share their charts in small share groups.

131 Yolen, Jane (1993). *Welcome to the Green House.* Illustrated by Laura Regan. New York: Putnam.

Environmental Focus: Recognizing the metaphor that a rainforest is a greenhouse

This book introduces the ecology of a rainforest through a poem that is illustrated. Using the metaphor that the rainforest is a "hot green house," reader will see some of the inhabitants — a blue hummingbird, a golden toad, waking lizards, a "plunge" of silver fish, and others. K–3.

Target Activity: "Inside a Hot Green Rainforest"

With children, review the closeup illustrations of animals and ask them to recreate the animal sounds in the poem. Use a map or globe to show children where the rainforests of the world are. Explain to them that the rainforests of the world are gradually being cut down, or deforested. Ask children to imagine what will happen to the rainforest inhabitants as the rainforest, their home, begins to disappear.

Literature for Grades 4–8

Realistic Contemporary Fiction

Realistic contemporary fiction — an author's writing that reflects people's lives in today's time period — tells readers that everything in the story "could" have happened to real people in today's real world. The writing focuses on the problems people face, how they cope, and the ways they are "human" in modern society. Realistic fiction can reassure older readers that they aren't the first ones to have a certain problem, and that they can vicariously experience situations that book characters have dealt with — in realistic situations. Realistic fiction related to the environment can help older children understand the realities of caring for the environment and coming to terms with the human problems and relationships that are involved in issues such as the ends of the spotted owl habitat versus the economic survival of the logging communities. Moreover, caring for the environment through the field of ecology can be merged in the classrooms of today with environmental science as portrayed in literature.

There are, for example, recent portrayals of people's tender feelings toward creatures in science stories related to biological life. *Fire Bug Connection: An Ecological Mystery* by Jean Craighead George is a fictional account of a caring, concerned twelve-year-old who examines clues with scientific reasoning and computer resources to solve the mystery of her dying fire bugs. The book also provides relevant information about the scientific method for the beginning ecologist.

Additional stories about people's love for the land, people sensing the spirit of living creatures, about appreciating the beauty of nature, and understanding the life of a paleontologist and other scientists are found in the following bibliography.

Grades 4–8

132 Ashabranner, Brent (1989). *Born to the Land: An American Portrait.* Photographs by Paul Conklin. New York: Putnam.
   Environmental Focus: Appreciating the impact of geography on the development of an area
   People—women and men, old and young, minorities, old-timers and newcomers—from Luna County, New Mexico, are interviewed. A reader learns about the relationship of generations, the effect of history on the present, the impact of geography on the development of the area, and the always-present threat of drought. Interviewees love the land and are willing to struggle to make a living from it. A sense of humor shows in anecdotes from the people that send meaningful messages: "if you wear out a pair of boots in this country, you will never leave" and "if you stay that long, you won't have enough money to leave." 4 up.
   Target Activity: "Ruining the Land"
   Create a large mural on butcher paper of a "natural" area complete with wildlife, trees, mountains, streams, and so forth, but with no human development. After completing the mural, brainstorm with the children a list of things that could happen if a much-needed energy source such as oil, coal, or uranium were to be discovered in that area. Have children draw pictures of these activities and facilities with one picture for each item that is listed. When all the pictures are completed, place them in the appropriate places on the mural. For example, have children put the pictures where they think the pictures would go if they were the energy developers. Let them pin, tack, or tape the pictures to the mural. Discuss the positive and negative impacts of the "new development" on the environment and wildlife, and create a list of these effects. Then, have children redevelop the energy source to see if they can come up with ways that the development could have less of an impact on the environment, yet still get the energy that is needed at an affordable cost. Further, have children look for similar situations in your area and report what they find back to the whole group.

133 Baylor, Byrd (1976). *Hawk, I'm Your Brother.* Illustrated by Peter Parnall. New York: Scribner's Sons.
   Environmental Focus: Appreciating the characteristics of birds
   Finding a hawk's nest in the Santos Mountains, Rudy Soto steals a baby redtail hawk in hopes he can learn how to fly, something he has always wanted to do. Realizing that the hawk resents being a captive in a cage, Rudy reluctantly frees the bird. As the hawk soars overhead, Rudy senses the spirit of the

hawk, flies with it in spirit, and they call to one another as one brother would call to another brother. 3–5.

Target Activity: "Sensing the Spirit of the Hawk"

Ask the children what the phrase "spirit of the hawk" means to them and write their responses on the board. Then reread the excerpt where Rudy releases the bird and feels he is flying with the bird in spirit. Invite individuals to tell how they would have felt if they had been there to "sense the spirit of the free creature" and encourage them to give reasons for their responses.

Additionally, discuss with children that in this book, and in another Baylor book, *The Desert Is Theirs* (Charles Scribner's Sons, 1975), the relationship between humans and earth shown through the Papago Indian culture emphasizes sharing with the earth and not taking from it. With children, discuss the theme: it points out what humans can learn from the animals and plants that adapt to the sun and to scarce water supply in the desert. How does the theme of learning from nature relate to the earlier Baylor story?

134 Byars, Betsy (1970). *Summer of the Swans.* Illustrated by Ted Conis. New York: Viking.

Environmental Focus: Appreciating the beauty of nature's creatures

As she moves into adolescence, Sara begins to see life as a series of "huge and uneven steps." She finds her mood swings overwhelming, for example, and begins to worry about her physical appearance — namely that her feet appear to be too large for her body. In the middle of Sara's struggle with her own feelings of loneliness and awkwardness, Sara's brother Charlie, who is mentally retarded, becomes lost one night when he leaves his home to visit some swans who have settled in a nearby pond. From the beginning of the summer when the story begins, to the end of the story at summer's end, the reader can follow Sara's growth of understanding of herself and her depth of caring for her brother. Charlie's disappearance allows Sara to come to terms with what is important in her life, and by facing the problem squarely, gives her newfound confidence in her own abilities. 5–6.

Target Activity: "Appreciating Nature's Creatures as a Writing Theme"

Mention to students that the title about the swans has significance as it points to the positive vision of life that is woven throughout the book. The swans change their resting pond, which attracts Charlie and leads Sara to search for him, and then, to find herself in the process of looking for him. When she discovers Charlie, Sara knows that she has found more than a frightened lost brother; she has found herself and changed her self-concept from that of an ugly duckling — someone who is too tall, unattractive, and clumsy

Grades 4–8

with her large feet — into one who feels more swanlike and content to be where she is instead of flying "away from everything, like the swans to a new lake." As in Andersen's story of *The Ugly Duckling*, Sara's self-concept is what changes — a change from believing she is a tall, clumsy person who is unattractive, to believing she is a capable, self-assured young woman. Ask children if they can think of other books that have nature's creatures as themes. Bring these in for a classroom display to interest children in further reading and browsing.

Optional Activity: "Imagery from Nature"

Summer of the Swans can be discussed for both content and writing style. This story of a mentally disabled brother offers possibilities for follow-up discussion: understanding a handicapped youngster, and exploring attitudes toward this condition; discovering examples of imagery; examining plot development and the growth of Sara's characterization. Further, students may review the story to find evidence of family interaction, discuss sensory experiences, look for art ideas, discuss different points of view, talk about the character's feelings or relate the story to personal feelings.

135 Conrad, Pam (1989). *My Daniel.* New York: Harper & Row.

Environmental Focus: Understanding the work of a paleontologist

Julia Creath Summerwaite (80 years old) flies to New York to visit her son's family and to take her grandchildren to the Natural History Museum. Verbal flashbacks from past to present link the story together. Summerwaite tells of her love for her older brother Daniel, his love for fossils, his search for a dinosaur, and the competitive nature of paleontologists for the fossils found in Nebraska. At the museum, the children learn of the harshness of pioneer life and the life of their Great-Uncle Daniel. 5 up.

Target Activity: "Being a Paleontologist"

With the students, discuss some of the following aspects of paleontology related to the story. Search for discoveries. Go on a newspaper search and begin to collect all the articles you can find about fossil discoveries in the United States. Allow yourself several weeks and use as many different papers (magazines, reports on television) as you can find. After you have collected and mounted your fossil articles in a scrapbook, how will you respond to the following:

    a. If you were to write a definition for the words "dinosaur hunter" what would it be?

    b. Find out all you can about one of our real-life dinosaur hunters and fossil-finders and ask, What has this scientist found? What have we learned from his or her findings? Look for resources with facts about Jim Jensen, Robert Owen and others.

c. What kinds of differences do you think there are between a person who is competitive in the search for fossils and one who is harmfully aggressive?

136 George, Jean Craighead (1993). *Fire Bug Connection: An Ecological Mystery.* Illustrated by Dan Brown. New York: HarperCollins.

Environmental Focus: Learning about the heroes and heroines of the environmental movement

On her annual summer trip with her parents to a mountain research laboratory in Maine, Maggie Mercer, an enthusiastic naturalist, collects insects and observes wildlife behavior while her parents study soil and plants. Maggie meets a graduate student from Czechoslovakia who gives her a terrarium of fire bugs for her twelfth birthday. When the exotic bugs begin to die after their fifth molting, Maggie realizes that something or someone is killing them. Maggie and her friend Mitch, a computer hacker, examine every possible clue with scientific reasoning and computer databases. Through this story, readers will see how individuals can have a large impact on the course of events that affect this planet. 6–8.

Target Activity: "Insects in Our Environment"

After reading George's book and discussing some of the included myths about the raven, the ramifications of global warming, and information about field methods of study, discuss the positive and negative things that insects can do for us. Ask the students to select an insect that is found in the area and find out what contribution it makes to the ecological system. What animals or other insects use it as a food source? Have the students interview local farmers, plant nursery suppliers, or gardeners to discover if their insect is considered a helper or a nuisance.

Optional Activity: "Using Scientific Reasoning to Solve an Ecological Mystery"

Review the background of the ecological mystery with the students, i.e., a graduate student gives Maggie a terrarium of exotic and brightly colored fire bugs; the fire bug larvae become unusually large after their fifth molt; and instead of changing into adults, they explode. Ask students to meet and discuss this with partners and write down the ways they would "attack" this mystery. For example, the partners can discuss such questions as, What elements of the problem should be explored? And why? If X happens, then what could be done? If Y happens, what should be explored further?

137 George, Jean Craighead (1972). *Julie of the Wolves.* New York: Harper & Row.
   Environmental Focus: Establishing a friendship with Nature's creatures
   Thirteen-year-old Julie-Miyax, an Eskimo girl, leaves her father-selected husband, Daniel, to cross the Tundra toward Point Hope where she plans to leave for San Francisco to find a California pen pal, Amy. Lost, Julie survives because of her knowledge of Eskimo lore (setting her course by migrating birds and the North Star) and her friendship with Amaroq, the leader of a wolf pack. 6–10.
   Target Activity: "Items for Survival"
   Considering the way that students live today, they should have little or no use for many of the items that are listed below. The teacher asks the girls and boys to imagine that they are caught in a snowstorm in the tundra, lose their way, and feel lost and become "marooned" on the ice and snow. There are no other human inhabitants—just Julie's Wolf Pack. Ask the students to participate in value ranking and to put the numbers 1, 2, 3, and so on in a priority order related to the items a student feels are necessary for him or her to survive in this situation.

Items for Survival

_____a dog sled   _____flintstone
_____spear   _____clothes
_____bow and arrow   _____hut, cabin, other shelter
_____knife   _____fence
_____dishes   _____signal device (flashlight)
_____food and water   _____fishhook and line
_____pet   _____snowshoes
_____firewood

138 George, Jean Craighead (1990). *On the Far Side of the Mountain.* Illustrated by the author. New York: E. P. Dutton.
   Environmental Focus: Appreciating the life of a rugged mountain dweller
   In their home environment on the mountain, Sam and his friend Bando search for Alice. During the search, they discover a ring of illegal falcon dealers. Told in first-person narrative using journal entries similar to those in *My*

Side of the Mountain (Dutton, 1988), with personal observations and growth in Sam's character. As a mountain dweller, Sam constructs devices to make their rugged life easier. Sam prepares and stores food, tans and sews deer hide, and carves. 4–6.

Target Activity: "Sam's Needs/Sam's Curiosity"

Initiate a discussion by asking students to recall the inventions Sam creates to make his rugged life in the mountains easier. With student volunteers writing on the board, the ideas are listed. The teacher invites discussion about each device with the question, How can you argue that this device was made because of Sam's practical needs (solving a problem) or with consideration of the environment?

Introduce *Birds* (Blackbirch Press, 1993) by Edward R. Riccluti, one of a series from Our Living World, to encourage the students to discover some of the patterns common to living things. Some of the patterns include ways living things react to stimuli, ways they reproduce, ways they adapt and what metabolism they have. Point out that living things share similar biological functions and that nature has a connectedness that includes humans as part of nature's network of life. Other titles in this series include *Insects, Mammals,* and *Fish*.

139 Hamilton, Virginia (1974). *M. C. Higgins, the Great.* New York: Macmillan.

Environmental Focus: Getting acquainted with the effects of mountain stripmining

Living on Sarah Mountain near the Ohio River, M. C. sees an enormous spoil heap left by stripminers. The spoil heap oozes slowly down the hill heading toward the house of his family. This place has been home to his family since 1854, when his great-grandmother Sarah, a runaway slave, found refuge on it. His father refuses to accept the danger of the landslide, and M. C. realizes he must save the family. To divert the slide, he builds a wall of earth reinforced with branches, old automobile fenders and a gravestone. M. C. interacts with his family; Ben Killburn, a child of a family shunned by the neighbors; Luhretta Outlaw, a strange girl; and James K. Lewis, who travels through the hills and records folksongs on his tape recorder. Advanced 6 up.

Target Activity: "Danger from a Landslide"

With the girls and boys, discuss the meaning of the word "danger" and its meaning in the story. Invite the students to reflect upon the phrase "danger from a landslide" and predict the effects of a landslide on the lives of the family. How would they have helped M. C. if they had been there? Ask the students to relate the story to contemporary times and their lives by telling the whole group about any incidents where there was "danger" in the environment (fast currents in local river where children swim or an avalanche, for example) and what they did to respond to the danger.

140 Hughes, Monica (1993). *The Crystal Drop.* New York: Simon & Schuster.

Environmental Focus: Becoming aware of the possibility of future drought situations

In southern Alberta in the year 2011, Megan, a teenager, sees her neighbors leave because the water supply is dwindling and turning the area into a burning desert. Global warming and a hole in the ozone have contributed to this dire situation. Megan's father abandons his family, and when her mother dies in childbirth, Megan and her ten-year-old brother Ian leave to walk west to her Uncle Greg's community of Gaia near Lundbreck Falls in the foothills of the Canadian Rockies. They meet descendants of the Blackfoot people and survivalists who guard their water with loaded guns. People are competing for the scarce resource. Both Megan and Ian begin to comprehend the ecological disaster but struggle on. 5–10.

Target Activity: "What Could Be the Ecological Disaster of Scarce Water?"

With students, discuss daily, weekly, or monthly activities that require water and write the students' remarks on the board. Write a heading, Things We Do That Require Water, and write their ideas under it on the lefthand side of the board. Then, ask students to predict for each of their ideas what would be changed or eliminated in their quality of life if there were no water or if water were scarce. Record their predictions under a heading, Predictions. Ask students to illustrate one or more of their illustrations for a class book or display.

Things We Do That Require Water	*Predictions*
1.	1.
2.	2.
3.	3.

141 Kidd, Nina (1991). *June Mountain Secret.* Illustrated by the author. New York: HarperCollins.

Environmental Focus: Appreciating the beauty of living creatures

This is a day's adventure at the McCloud River for little Jenny and her father, as the two work hard to land a beautiful rainbow trout, and then set it free so it can return to its habitat in the cool river water. Shows the beauty of the river habitat and the creatures living in the water. Drawings of life in the habitat included. 4–6.

Target Activity: "Aquatic Habitats"

Pick two aquatic habitats, such as lake and river, or pond and stream, or fresh water and salt water. Make or cut out drawings or pictures of aquatic animals for each habitat, putting each animal on a separate card or piece of paper. Mix them all together. Allow one child at a time to see if she or he can sort them out — correctly, identifying which animals live in which aquatic habitats. Do any seem to live in both? If yes, which ones? Create a poster display to show the variety of animals that live in each of these two aquatic environments.

Optional Activity: "Secrets in Illustrations of the Environment"

With an opaque projector, review the illustrations with the students and point out some of the details, such as the way the author portrayed the running water of the river, used different shades of the same color for a natural effect, and presented images of the life cycle of the mayfly as it changed from its larva stage to the adult stage. Invite students to connect the illustrations of the river setting with wading in a cold river, fishing, or any of their other experiences, and tell about them.

142 King-Smith, Dick (1993). *The Cuckoo Child*. Illustrated by Leslie Bowman. New York: Hyperion.

Environmental Focus: Appreciating the value of releasing a captive creature into the wild

Since he was a preschooler, eight-year-old Jack Daw has been fascinated by raising barnyard fowl and by any other creature that had feathers. He still has this fascination, and while on a class trip to a wildlife park, he takes an ostrich egg. He tries to hatch it by putting the eight-inch "cuckoo" egg under a brooding goose. When hatched, the "gosling" is VERY large and quite strange looking, but the family and the animals accept this odd-looking creature. Finally, when the bird is nine feet tall two years later, Jack realizes that the bird needs other ostriches and returns him to the wildlife park. There, the young ostrich first sees his own kind. 4–5.

Target Activity: "Returning an Animal to the Wild"

With children, discuss the dilemma Jack faced when he realized that the "cuckoo" bird needed other ostriches and that he had to return him to the wild. Ask children why wild animals should be returned to the wild and discuss

Grades 4–8

some of the problems that arise when a wild animal has depended on humans for food and then is turned loose in the wild. Ask children to take the role of Jack and meet with partners to portray what Jack said to his best friend when he realized his dilemma. Ask children to trade roles. Further, ask children to consider what happened when the young ostrich saw his own species for the first time and realized who he was. Finally ask children to illustrate what they think happened to the ostrich after he was returned to the wild.

143 Klass, David (1994). *California Blue*. New York: Scholastic.

Environmental Focus: Protecting endangered species

His father is dying of leukemia and John spends his long distance runs sorting out his feelings for a man with whom he has nothing in common. Their relationship has always been rocky. Now that there seems to be little time left, John feels guilty and angry that they haven't gotten along better. His irascible father hasn't made things easy. During one of his training runs on the property of the local lumber mill, John finds a beautiful blue butterfly, unlike any he has ever seen. Should he publicize his exciting discovery? If the government decides to protect this new species by closing down the mill, John will not only incur the wrath of the townspeople but his father's as well. If he saves the butterfly, he must be willing to abandon any hope of reconciliation with his father. This compelling novel looks at the passion on both sides of a volatile ecological issue, and explores — both emotionally and economically — the price of fighting for one's beliefs. 6–8

Target Activity: "What Would *You* Do?"

Have children research some of the species living in your area that are currently on the endangered species list. Ask children to select one of these species and write a story detailing a fictional problem animal has when people interfere with its habitat. Encourage children to explain in their stories what they would do to defend the species in a way that is similar — or different from — the approach John took.

144 Locker, Thomas (1986). *Sailing with the Wind*. Illustrated by the author. New York: Dial Books.

Environmental Focus: Appreciating the changing moods of the wind

Sailing with the Wind is a beautifully simple tale of a young girl who goes sailing with her favorite uncle. As they travel down the river, the land, water,

Realistic Contemporary Fiction

and sky change constantly. The fog vanishes in the morning as the sun and wind come up; clouds pass into thunderclouds, but the storm never materializes and the flowing sunset is serene upon the river. When she returns home, the girl has tasted the shifting moods and colors of nature and is changed—as is the reader. The art for each picture consists of an oil painting which is camera-separated and reproduced in full-color, adding immeasurably to the text. 4–6.

Target Activity: "Uses of the Wind"

Discuss the relative advantages of using sailboats versus motorized boats. What effects do both have on the environment? Have children interview both a sailboat owner and an owner of a motorized craft and solicit their input about the advantages and disadvantages of both kinds of boats. Invite children to share the results of the interviews with the boat owners and discuss what they learned. Finally, ask children how they think the feeling of the book would have changed if the boat had been a motorized craft. Why do they think so?

145 Markle, Sandra (1993). *Outside and Inside Trees.* New York: Bradbury.

Environmental Focus: Appreciating trees

A well-organized text supported by close-up photographs, clear captions, a pronunciation guide, and a glossary/index offers many interesting facts about trees and how they grow. The pictures of very young children throughout the text are misleading, however, because the book is appropriate for a much older audience. 3–6

Target Activity: "Arbor Day Celebration"

Plan now for an Arbor Day Celebration next April. Some students may want to research Arbor Day's beginning and its exact date for their area of the country, while others might want to plan an observance with information about trees and perhaps create a reader's theatre script or an original play based on a forest theme. The play could be put on for the community; with the proceeds, purchase trees to be planted on the school ground. For information on Arbor Day, write:

> National Arbor Day Foundation
> 100 Arbor Avenue
> Nebraska City, NE 68410

Grades 4–8

146 Page, Valerie King (1970). *Pi Gal.* Illustrated by Jacques Callaert. New York: Dodd, Mead & Co.

Environmental Focus: Understanding ways of interacting with an island environment

In Page's story, Prince Williams is a young boy growing up on Cat Island, an Outer Island in the Bahamas. Like many other children on the island, he longs for a chance to live a more exciting life in exotic places far beyond the island. While searching for his lost dog, he comes upon two divers who have come to the island to salvage a lost barge. Prince soon learns to dive, and the beautiful underwater life of the reef is revealed to him for the first time. After many frustrating attempts, Prince finds the barge they have been seeking and, at the same time, discovers he is a talented diver and decides to pursue diving as a career. 5–6.

Target Activity: "Underwater Life Resources Book"

Invite students to consider the idea that a coral reef is a bounty of underwater resources; there are many valuables there that each student may or may not know about. Explain that people must keep searching to find what makes the resources in a reef unique and special. Write on the chalkboard the following expository frame:

Once I didn't know this information about a coral reef: _____.
But now I know that _____.
And I want to learn more about _____.

Fill in the lines as a group, allowing many students to contribute ideas for the blanks. Next, encourage students to write their own underwater resource poems, illustrating them if they so desire. Collect the poems and put them into a class Underwater Resources Book. Put the book on display so that all can see what their classmates know and someday hope to learn about the value of a coral reef and its inhabitants.

147 Paterson, Katherine (1977). *Bridge to Terabithia.* Illustrated by Donna Diamond. New York: Harper & Row.

Environmental Focus: Appreciating the beauty of an imagined special environment

In Paterson's story, Jess Aarons is a ten-year-old boy growing up in rural Virginia with what he describes as "a great piece missing" because of his fear of swinging across a high creek on a rope. He has formed an unlikely friendship with Leslie Burke, a little girl whose family has left the city for a better way of life. Leslie's life is filled with books and imagination, and together the two create Terabithia, their secret kingdom in the woods where magical, beautiful things happen routinely through the forces of their imaginations.

Jess admires Leslie because she not only has led him to this magical world, but she seems to have no fears of anything. When Leslie is killed crossing the creek to Terabithia, Jess uses all that Leslie has taught him to enable him to cope with the unexpected tragedy. Jess' friendship with Leslie and her family shows him a new, more positive way to live. With the death of Leslie, he brings his little sister into Terabithia, which helps to assuage his pain. He also begins to share his new values with his family. 4 up.

Target Activity: "The Natural Beauty of a Special Kingdom"

Ask students to describe the natural beauty of Terabithia, the world that Leslie and Jess created. Ask them if they have ever made up a fictional place. What was it like? Have children form small groups and create a fantasy world with related natural beauty and have them develop the rules in their special places. Ask them to make group decisions to do the following:

1. Who will be allowed to enter your kingdom?
2. What are the rules in your kingdom? What are the rules related to maintaining natural beauty?
3. What natural creatures live in your kingdom?
4. What is the natural beauty in your kingdom?

Children may want to draw a mural of their kingdoms. Additionally, encourage them to "discover" their kingdoms outside of school.

148 Peake, Katy (1972). *The Indian Heart of Carrie Hodges.* Illustrated by Thomas B. Allen. New York: Viking Press.

Environmental Focus: Appreciating animals and nature in a desert environment

Carrie Hodges is a serious and sensitive little girl who loves animals and nature. Growing up in the desert environment of Southern California, she has come to appreciate the flora and fauna around her. She is befriended by a desert-seasoned old recluse, Foster, who shares her love of nature and begins teaching her about the Indian ways and the magical relations that once existed between the Indians and the animals. Carrie is tormented when the ranchers in the valley decide to kill all the coyotes in the area because one coyote killed some sheep. She sets out on a mission to save the coyotes and learns about her own animal spirit at the same time. Carrie's special relationship with Foster is highlighted in this book. Their common love of nature brings them close, and the old man teaches her all he can from his lifetime of solitary observation. 5–6.

Grades 4–8

Target Activity: "Research about Animals in Nature"

Tell students that they are going to do a very interesting kind of research. They are going to research animals "by finding out everything they can about five wild animals of their choice." Explain that they may use any sources available to find out what these animals are really like — zoologists, encyclopedias, Indian legends, videotapes, etc. When the five animals have been researched, ask children to write an essay describing which animal they appreciate the most and why this is so. Finally, have pairs of children share their essays with one another. Provide an opportunity for children to tell how their essay compares with their partner's description of the animal they appreciate the most.

149 Pitseolak, Peter (1977). *Peter Pitseolak's Escape from Death.* Introduced and edited by Dorothy Eber. New York: Delacorte Press/Seymour Lawrence.

Environmental Focus: Getting acquainted with ways people face the forces of nature

On a walrus hunt in his canoe with his son, Peter Pitseolak, an Eskimo artist of Baffin Island, finds himself stranded in a huge ice field that is moving swiftly out to sea. After two nights on the ice, a bluebird appears to Peter in a strange dream. The dream gives Peter courage and hope that they will find a path through the ice field and return to safety. The wind that Peter once feared drives their canoe back toward Baffin Island. Peter notes in this retrospective story, "There is nothing in the world that is not good. I understood this then." The story is related as a firsthand account by the author. He poignantly portrays his fear of never seeing his family again, which is contrasted with his renewed feeling of hope and optimism after the dream. 4–6.

Target Activity: "Nature's Obstacle or Challenge?"

Write on the chalkboard the following sentence from Peter Pitseolak's Escape from Death: "There is nothing in the world that is not good." Ask students to tell what they think Peter meant by this statement in the context of his harrowing experience in the environment. Point out the idea that a harsh environment presents some very difficult situations that may seem overwhelming and unfair at the time, but the situations often bring us new understandings about ourselves and the world. These situations may bring new friends or, in some other ways, turn out to be positive challenges. Write on the chalkboard, "Nature's Obstacle or Challenge?" and invite students to share some past experience that first seemed like an obstacle, but later, in retrospect, they could view as a positive challenge, because it had benefits. After all who wish to have shared orally, ask students to select one event to describe in essay format using the title, "Nature's Obstacle or Challenge?"

150 Slepian, Jan (1990). *Risk n' Roses.* New York: Philomel.
   Environmental Focus: Recognizing that flowers convey meanings to people
   In a new neighborhood, Skip wants to be accepted into Jean Persico's gang. The girls have a secret club and each must meet a challenge stated by Persico. Persico is a pest and torments old Mr. Kaminsky, who has befriended Skip's retarded sister, Angela, but who has no use for the gang leader. Sensing Skip's rejection, Jean talks Angela into cutting the flowers from all of Mr. Kaminsky's prize roses, another one of her torments. Skip stops being mesmerized by Jean and decides to go her own way. 5–7.
   Target Activity: "Roses That Have Meaning for People"
   You can set the stage for discussing ways that flowers in general have meaning for people, as well as ways that flowers, specifically Mr. Kaminsky's roses, had meaning for the characters in the story. What meaning did the prize roses have for:
   1. Mr. Kaminsky, an elderly man, who spent a great deal of time growing the prize roses.
   2. Angela, a retarded girl, who became a friend of Mr. Kaminsky.
   3. Angela's sister, Skip, who finally rejected the female gang leader, Jean Persico.
   4. Jean Persico, who felt Skip's rejection and got her sister, Angela, in trouble by talking Angela into cutting the flowers from all of the old man's prize roses.
   Optional Activity: "An Environmental Club"
   Ask the students to imagine that everyone in the class is a member of a secret club that is supportive and positive about everything in the environment. In the group, each student prints her name on a paper that is passed to the right (or left) of the person next to her. Each student in turn writes something positive that the student has done for the environment. After passing the papers to all in the class in turn, each student receives her own sheet back to keep as a record of the contributions to the environment and as her initiation into the class club about environment.

Grades 4–8

151 Stopl, Hans (1990). *The Golden Bird.* Illustrated by Lidia Postma. New York: Dial.

Environmental Focus: Recognizing that the cycles in nature can be reassuring

Eleven-year-old Daniel is hospitalized with cancer. He sees three birds on the sill: one green, one blue and one golden. The blue bird brings messages from the golden bird daily — messages that say, "Watch the tree outside your window. It may look dead to you, but if you look more closely, you'll see buds on it." Daniel discusses death with his mother and the nurses and, lovingly and honestly, they help him face it. Realistic scenes include the hospital, his mother at the bedside, nurses caring for him, and visitors talking with Daniel. Realistic yet reassuring approach for those who face the death of a terminally ill child. 4 up.

Target Activity: "Reflowering of the Cherry Tree"

Daniel comes to see death as a transformation similar to the reflowering of the cherry tree outside his window. Family love supports the story as reader sees the nature of death. In small response groups, encourage children to consider: What opinions do you have about the situation which developed where the blue bird brings messages daily from the golden bird to Daniel? What do you think Daniel means when he says death is a transformation similar to the reflowering of the cherry tree? Each group asks a volunteer to report on the group's considerations when all the students return together as a total group.

152 Strachan, Ian (1990). *The Flawed Glass.* New York: Little, Brown.

Environmental Focus: Appreciating creatures in an island environment

On an island off Scotland, Shona MacLeod and her family, who appreciate nature and the island creatures, face poachers and engage in conflict with the new American owners of the island. Shona, physically handicapped and unable to walk or talk, is mentally clear but cannot tell others her thoughts. When she rescues Carl, the owner's son, from a potentially fatal accident, the two become friends. As new friends, Carl teaches Shona to use his dad's computer and Shona shows Carl the birds of the island — in particular, the eagle hatchlings who, like Shona, also struggle for survival. Together they see other wonders of nature on the island. 5–6.

Target Activity: "Researching the Wonders of Nature"

Have students form small groups based upon their selection of a natural wonder in the book about which they would like to know more. Provide encyclopedias and other data sources so that the students can write brief research reports on their selected topic. For example, some students may select the topic of eagles when they recall that Shona's struggles to walk and talk were the survival techniques she faced that were compared by the author with the ways the eagle babies struggled to live and survive. The students' research reports can include facts about the eagle's diet, eggs laid by the female, habitat, migration habits, and its prey and predators.

153 Vieira, Linda (1994). *The Ever-Living Tree: The Life and Times of a Coast Redwood.* Illustrated by Christopher Canyon. New York: Walker.
Environmental Focus: Understanding the growth of a tree
Vieira and Canyon deftly blend the stages of growth of a coast redwood tree with an account of major epochs in world history. A timeline advances across the top of each double-page spread, while insets and border illustrations enrich this outstanding informational book.
Target Activity: "A Tree's Timeline"
Using Vieira's book, the students might want to try to find the oldest tree on their school grounds or neighborhood. Then they could estimate its age and construct a timeline of historical events that occurred during the tree's lifetime, including major world, national, and local events.

154 Wildsmith, Brian (1967). *Birds.* Illustrated by the author. New York: Franklin Watts.
Environmental Focus: Showing an appreciation for birds
As explained in the preface to this delightful book, some people collect words that refer to a collection of creatures ("a party of jays") the way others collect stamps or antique bottles. This book shows beautifully illustrated birds in congregations — with the colloquial names given to the bird flocks over the years. The book provides a joyful blend of bird study and wordplay. 2–3.
Target Activity: "Bird Study"
Have children form small groups based upon their selection of a bird about which they would like to know more. Provide encyclopedias and other research materials so that children can write brief research reports on their bird, including such facts as migration patterns, habitat, diet, predators, and number of eggs laid.
Optional Activity: "A Birdfeeder"

Grades 4–8

Children can learn to identify birds, discover which birds eat which seeds, and determine which kind of birds will come to a feeder at different times of the year. Hummingbird feeders draw especially delightful visitors. Tell children that birds can also teach different flight strategies — hovering versus gliding, for example — leading to discussions of how inventors get their ideas from nature.

155 Wildsmith, Brian (1982). *Pelicans.* Illustrated by the author. New York: Pantheon.

Environmental Focus: Getting acquainted with ways to care for a wild creature

Paul finds a little box that has fallen off a truck. Inside is an egg which he puts under his hen to hatch. After hatching, the little bird doesn't seem to like regular hen food and is nearly starved when Paul's father brings home four trout for their dinner and they notice the bird likes the trout. Paul brings the bird to the river but it doesn't know how to fish. His family threatens to take the bird, that they now realize is a pelican, to the zoo since he can't fish. One evening, Paul and the pelican watch a kingfisher dive into the water and catch fish; the pelican learns to catch his supper for the very first time. The bird flies away to the "land of the pelicans." Paul is sad, but he realizes the pelican will be really happy now. K–3.

Target Activity: "Learning to Be a Pelican"

Ask children how they learned to feed themselves and how eventually they were taught how to use a knife and fork (or chopsticks). Did someone have to teach them these skills? Would they have learned how to do these things if adults, or older children, had not shown them how? Discuss the problems the pelican had learning how to procure his own fish. Do most pelicans have this problem? Why not? Invite children to role-play the scene when Paul and the pelican watch the kingfisher and the pelican finally learns to fish for himself.

156 Zolotow, Charlotte (1972). *The Beautiful Christmas Tree.* Illustrated by Ruth Robbins. Oakland, CA: Parnassus Press.

Environmental Focus: Recognizing that all living things need love

Mr. Crockett's neighbors have beautifully ornamented Christmas trees, but he has a scraggly tiny potted pine tree in his brownstone house window. The neighbors are disgusted, and become even more so when he plants the ugly thing in front of his house the following spring. The lonely man knows

Realistic Contemporary Fiction

a wonderful secret, however: all living things need love. So as the seasons go by, the man cares for the tree, warming it with hay in the winter, and watering it in the summer. He puts out crumbs for the birds so that they come and feed and sing in the branches of the thriving tree. 4–6.

Target Activity: "Love and Caring Count"

Mr. Crockett, through his love and caring for a scraggly tree, made the earth a healthier place. In the following situations where people have hurt the environment, have students discuss how love and caring might have made a difference:

1. A couple of people take a walk and one throws a soda bottle away in the woods. A mouse crawls in but can't get out. It dies there.

2. A machine in a factory pumps waste into a nearby river. The fish in the river die from pollution. An osprey flying over cannot find any fish for food.

3. Someone tosses a lighted cigarette out of a car window. It lands in some papers along the side of the road and they burst into flames. The fire spreads and a bird sitting on her nest nearby has to flee or get burned. Moles, mice and chipmunks also run for their lives.

Optional Activity: "Seasonal Changes"

Seasons, such as those depicted in the story, also teach children about cycles of life and death. Discuss the changes of the seasons. This can lead to a study of weather; a thermometer and a record book can teach children the rudiments of data collection. Scatter thermometers around your school yard to teach about temperature differences in shade, partial shade, and sun.

As a whole group, discuss the differences in temperatures. Compare these differences at different times of the year. Ask children: Which of these times of the year are associated with "life" and "growth"? Why? Which tend to be associated with "death"? Why?

(Zolotow)

Folk Literature

Folk literature — the simple fireside stories, the long epics, legends about heroes, and myths about gods, goddesses, and the creation of things — began in the stories, ballads, and other folk songs related to the oral tradition created by early people. This section discusses the folktales and fairy tales related to the oral traditions that are suitable for older children. Tales about the creation of things, about the time when the distinctions between animals and humans were blurred and they could understand one another or "speak the same language," and about the ways humans adapted to events in nature, are found in the following bibliography.

157 Bierhorst, John (1993). *The Woman Who Fell from the Sky: The Iroquois Story of Creation.* New York: Morrow.
   Environmental Focus: Getting acquainted with Native North Americans' appreciation of nature
   On an island in the sky lit by a shining tree, a woman and man live until the woman hears her children speaking from within her. In a jealous rage, the man uproots the tree and pushes her through the hole. Her fall to the water below is saved by birds and she lands on the back of a turtle. After creating the earth, stars, and sun, the Sky Woman has twin sons, Sapling and Flint. Sapling creates the animal and plant life and Flint creates water, snow and various monsters. Deciding to leave Earth, the twins take different routes and divide up the Milky Way while doing so. Sky Woman leaves and flies up to the sky on the fire's smoke and tells the Native People that their thoughts can also rise as she did. 4–6.
   Target Activity: "A Tribute of Thanks to Sky Woman"
   Show students the final page of the book that has the Native People's Tribute of Thanks to Sky Woman. Discuss the words and then return to the book to review the illustrations that portray this story of earth's creation and are so in keeping with the People's respect for nature in this Native American legend.

Folk Literature

Have children bring in other books that they know about that show the respect of Native Americans have for the land and things of nature.

158 Birrer, Cynthia, and William Birrer (1987). *Song to Demeter.* New York: Lothrop, Lee & Shepard.

Environmental Focus: Getting acquainted with our natural heritage in a Greek myth

This is the story of Demeter (Greek for Ceres), the goddess of agriculture including grain, harvest, fruits, flowers, and fertility of the earth. The story tells of seasonal changes. Hades, god of the underworld in this Greek myth, carries Demeter's daughter, Persephone, off to his land to be his bride. Demeter mourns for her daughter and asks Zeus to do something. She is told Persephone can return if she has eaten nothing in Hades. However, since she has eaten pomegranate seeds, she has to return to Hades for four months every year. The season of her absence is winter. 4–6.

Target Activity: "A Heritage from Demeter"

With interested students, introduce "A Heritage from Demeter" in the form of a Readers' Theater related to earth's ecological history. For example, engage students in identifying some environmental landmarks beginning in 1962 when Rachel Carson first wrote her book, *Silent Spring,* about the effects of pesticides on the environment. Then ask students to identify excerpts from their related readings to add to a script, or discuss with them a similar script that they write themselves.

If desired, ask students to set up a book display with various versions of the myth of Demeter that the students have located in the book corner or in the school library. Examples can include Margaret Hodges' *Persephone and the Springtime: A Greek Myth* (Little, Brown, 1973); Gerald McDermott's *Daughter of Earth: A Roman Myth* (Delacorte, 1984); Penelope Proddow's *Demeter and Persephone* (Doubleday, 1972); and Sarah Tomaino's *Persephone, Bringer of Spring* (Crowell, 1971).

159 Curry, Jane Louise, reteller (1987). *Back in the Beforetime: Tales of the California Indians.* Illustrated by James Watts. New York: Macmillan.

Environmental Focus: Getting acquainted with some world creation tales of Native Americans

Curry tells of the beforetime, when the world was newly made by Old

Grades 4–8

Man Above and when animals lived together as people. The stories are told as a chronicle and trace the world from its creation, to Coyote stealing the sun, to his first making of man, and then to the awakening of the first man. 4–6.

Target Activity: "Changes Came to the World"

Encourage students to think of some "changes that could come to the world that would help our planet environmentally." Ask students to print their thoughts on a paper and pass the papers to the right. Each student in turn writes something more about "changes that could come." Finally each student has his or her own "changes" sheet to keep. This is a list of written ideas for the student to use as a resource during the class's discussion about how to make this planet a better place for all of its inhabitants.

160 Goble, Paul, reteller (1978). *The Girl Who Loved Wild Horses.* Illustrated by the reteller. New York: Bradbury Press.

Environmental Focus: Fostering an understanding of the human-animal relationship of Native Americans

A girl goes down to the river at sunrise to watch the wild horses, rests in the meadow, and then sleeps. A thunderstorm rumbles and the girl joins the horses running away from a lightning flash and the gathering storm; she finally goes to live with them.

Once students understand the point of view that many Indian tales are handed down from a time when the distinctions between animals and humans were blurred, they realize that in the early beginnings of these tales, animals and humans could understand one another or "speak the same language." Thus, there is no distinction between animals and humans in some of the ancient Native American tales. 5–6.

Target Activity: "Humans Are the Keepers of the Earth and the Animals"

After reading the story aloud to students, mention that in many of the early Native American tales the distinctions between animals and humans were not made, and that in some tales, the animals and humans were as one people and could speak the same language and understand one another. Thus, it was no surprise when a human went to live with or married an animal in some of the tales. Remind the students of the Native American belief in the before-time, when the world was newly made by Old Man Above and when animals and people lived together. Discuss the point of view shown by this story and the ways it may differ in the points of view held by some children in the class.

Next, introduce two other books to show that the people believed they were the keepers of the earth and the animals; read excerpts from the stories in *Keepers of the Animals: Native American Stories and Environmental Activities for Children* (Fulcrum, 1991) and *Keepers of the Earth: Native American Stories and Environmental Activities for Children* (Fulcrum, 1988) both by Michael Caduto and Joseph Bruchac. Discuss several of the suggested environmental activities to encourage students to become interested in becoming "Earth-Keepers" and "Animal-Keepers."

161 Grifalconi, Ann (1986). *The Village of Round and Square Houses*. Illustrated by the author. Boston: Little, Brown.
  Environmental Focus: Getting acquainted with humans' adaptability to events in nature
  This book explains why the men in a Cameroon village, Tos, in central Africa live in square houses while the women live in round houses. One night long ago, the old Naka mountain volcano erupted and left only two houses standing in the village — one round and one square. To take care of the people while the village was being rebuilt, the village chief sent the tall men to live in the square house and the women to live in the round house. 4–6.
  Target Activity: "Retelling Stories of Events in Nature"
  Introduce storytelling about events in nature by encouraging students to use a story beginning such as "In the days of long, long ago," and storytelling endings such as "And that is how our way came about and why it will continue..." Ask the students to retell a story to one another in pairs. Have the students switch roles so all have a turn to say the storytelling beginnings and endings.

162 Levitt, Paul M., and Elissa S. Guralnick (1988). *The Stolen Appaloosa and Other Indian Stories*. Illustrated by Carolynn Roche. New York: Bookmakers Guild.
  Environmental Focus: Appreciating how seasons came to be through Native American stories
  This book has five tales from the Pacific Northwest Indian tribes. Mythic characters tell the story of how seasons come to change in "The Story of Hot and Cold," a tale to compare with the story of Demeter and Persephone. In another, a difficult winter is the setting for the story of a woman reunited with her people after her offspring become the hunters who provide food and save the village. 4–6.
  Target Activity: "Appreciating Tales of Seasonal Change"

Grades 4–8

Bring students together to discuss "The Story of Hot and Cold" and ask them if they know of similar stories about the reasons seasons change. Read the story of *Demeter and Persephone* and discuss the similarities between the two stories. Build a chart of information that compares points in the two stories and display it so that children can add information to it as they find additional stories. Review the stories again to look for evidence of traits of environmental awareness in the main characters. Add the information to the chart.

Similarities

Demeter and Persephone   The Story of Hot and Cold
1.
2.

163 Luenn, Nancy (1993). *Song for the Ancient Forest.* Illustrated by Jill Kastner. New York: Atheneum.

Environmental Focus: Understanding the significance of Native American tales about the creation of nature

Raven, also known as a trickster, predicted the destruction of the forest, made a song with the power to change this destruction, and sang it to the Original Native People, who laughed at both him and the song. Through history's different time periods, Raven sang his song to different people, but it wasn't until Raven sang the song to a small girl in today's world that someone understood the important message Raven was singing. The girl, the daughter of a timber logger, sang the song to her father, who sang it to other loggers and the landowner. When the landowner heard it, he angrily attacked Raven and wounded him. As a result, the blood from Raven's wound carried the song into every "living thing" before Raven was reborn in this tale.

Target Activity: "What Could Raven's Song Say about Nature?"

The author's well-intended message about the importance of conserving America's old-growth forests is clear and can be discussed with the students: Based on Raven's problem and his struggles to have the People consider the message in his song, what suggestions would you put into a song to portray nature? In groups, ask students to draw the outline of a raven on sheets of paper and write in their suggestions in the outlines. The suggestions may be read to partners and discussed. Further, a writer can choose the extent to which he wants to make the changes mentioned in the feedback. Revisions may be made before returning to a whole group situation where volunteers may read some of their suggestions for the song to the whole class. To dictate a complete song, invite students to suggest lines to be written on the board.

Folk Literature

The final version may be hand-copied into the students' notebooks about the environment.

164 Monroe, Jean Guard, and Ray A. Williamson (1987). *They Dance in the Sky: Native American Star Myths.* Illustrated by Edgar Stewart. Boston: Houghton Mifflin.

Environmental Focus: Getting acquainted with the significance of Native American tales about the stars

In the first two chapters, there are stories from many Native American groups about the Seven Sisters (the Pleiades) and the Big Dipper. The remaining chapters are divided by regions and tell different stories from the people of the different regions. The authors provide information about the people who told each story, as well as explanations of the story's symbolic significance. The book is decorated with black and white drawings of a variety of Indian symbols, of the constellations, and of animals and people, which lend additional meaning to the pages. A read aloud. Ages 4–8.

Target Activity: "Reading Aloud"

With the students, the teacher discusses the oral tradition in which such stories were originally passed along to others. The teacher may decide to save this one for the end of the school year as students begin to talk about going to day camp in town or away to camp in the country. After reading some of the selections, the teacher can encourage the students to take this book along (checked out from the library) with a chart of the skies to compare ideas about the constellations with the ideas presented in the Native American folk-tale.

Fanciful Fiction

Fanciful fiction — narratives that could not possibly happen in the real world as we know it — can provide fundamental environmental truths and new insights to readers. Older students, grades 4 and up, have several fanciful books to choose from that relate to caring for the environment.

An example of fanciful rendering, Monica Hughes's *The Crystal Drop* is set in southern Alberta in the year 2011, and is an account of Megan, a teenager, who sees her neighbors leave because the water supply is dwindling. The area is turning into a burning desert because of global warming and a hole in the ozone layer. The book provides many new ideas for readers to explore.

Reading quality fanciful fiction, exemplified by the following, will help an older reader develop his or her imagination, consider new ideas and alternative lifestyles, and get acquainted with unfamiliar faces and places.

165 Geisel, Theodore Seuss (1971). *The Lorax.* Illustrated by the author. New York: Random House.

Environmental Focus: Recognizing the need to care for the environment

In the delightful rhymed format of Dr. Seuss, we find the story of the Truffula Trees that provided shade, gave fruit, and added beauty to the earth. Then one day, someone chops down a Truffula Tree and, with its soft tuft, makes a Thneed. The Lorax, speaking for the trees, tells the man that he is "crazy with greed" and that no one will buy Thneeds, but they do. Factories are built to manufacture Thneeds. The environment becomes smoggy and the rivers dirty with the leftover "goo" from the factories. The last Truffula Tree is finally felled and the Lorax leaves with one word, "Unless," which means "Unless someone like you cares a whole lot, nothing is going to get better." 4–6.

Target Activity: "Foresters vs. the Environmentalists"

To ensure that children understand the analogies in the story, ask them to identify real-life examples of the following items in the story: "swomee-swans," "truffula-trees," "brown bar-ba-lds," "humming fish," "thneeds," "once-leers," "smogulous smolee," "gluppity-glupp," and "schlopity-schlopp."

A "thneed" is defined as a fine thing that everyone thinks that they need — perhaps a luxury. Ask children to name some examples of thneeds in contemporary life. Ask them also how the "once-lers" could have made the "thneeds" without destroying the environment.

Finally, it is important that children not walk away from this book with the one-sided view that trees should not be cut down. Rather, they can be made aware that the key is managing and harvesting our resources wisely to get the best use out of any resources that we utilize. Reducing consumption, reusing materials, and recycling resources are some ways that children can help.

To graphically illustrate both sides of this issue, have them prepare for a debate. One side will be the foresters who earn their living by logging. The other side is the environmentalists, who are only interested in saving the forests. Have both sides research their position using old newspapers and magazines, and then choose three representatives from each side to conduct the debate. To summarize, help the two sides reach a compromise based on lowering the number of trees felled, and the reusing and recycling of wood products.

166 Hughes, Monica (1993). *The Crystal Drop*. New York: Simon & Schuster.

Environmental Focus: Recognizing importance of water to humans

In southern Alberta in the year 2011, Megan, a teenager, sees her neighbors leave because the water supply is dwindling and turning the area into a burning desert. Global warming and a hole in the ozone have contributed to this dire situation. Megan's father abandons his family, and when her mother dies in childbirth, Megan and her ten-year-old brother, Ian, leave to walk west to her Uncle Greg's community of Gaia near Lundbreck Falls in the foothills of the Canadian Rockies. They meet descendants of the Blackfoot people and survivalists who guard their water with loaded guns. Both Megan and Ian begin to comprehend the ecological disaster, but they struggle on. 5–10.

Target Activity: "A Personal Water Conservation Plan"

Have children "guess-ti-mate" the amount of water they use daily, beginning with a list of all the activities they participate in that require water usage. Then share with them the following chart:

Grades 4–8

WATER INFORMATION SHEET

brushing teeth (with water running)	3 gallons
cleaning the house	8 gallons
cooking three meals	8 gallons
flushing the toilet	3–5 gallons
taking a bath	30–40 gallons
taking a shower	5 gallons per minute
washing a car	30–40 gallons
washing clothes	20–30 gallons
washing dishes	10 gallons
watering a lawn	30–40 gallons
miscellaneous	?

Have students now revise their original estimates using this new information. Most students will be amazed. Ask them to then keep track of how much water is used in their homes for five days. Suggest that a sheet be posted on the refrigerator and that each family member help by putting an X in the section designated on the sheet after each case of water use.

After the water use data has been gathered, make a master chart that summarizes the total use in the classroom for the five-day period. Challenge each child to create a "Personal Water Conservation Plan" to intentionally reduce his or her water usage and invite their families to join in on the plan.

167 Spinner, Stephanie (1994). *Aliens for Dinner.* New York: Random House.

Environmental Focus: Stopping pollution

A bossy extraterrestrial named Aric has popped out of Richard's fortune cookie with urgent news: a group of pollution-loving aliens named the Dwibs are getting ready to turn planet Earth into a Toxic Waste Theme Park. Their only hope is to incapacitate the invaders with a fatal case of boredomitis at the opening ceremonies for the new recycling plant. Can they find someone really boring in time? The principal of Richard's school may have the answer. Fast-paced hilarity to delight newly-independent readers. 1–4.

Target Activity: "A Toxic Waste Theme Park"

On the blackboard or overhead, write the words "Toxic Waste Theme Park." Ask children to brainstorm some pollution-causing practices that might be highlighted at such a place. Using a large sheet of butcher paper and tempera paints, encourage children to paint scenes depicting people engaged in

Fanciful Fiction

these various earth-unfriendly activities, making each one an amusement park ride, concession games, or other attractions that one would be likely to see at a theme park. Place the butcher paper across a wall in the back of the classroom and refer to it in a discussion of the dangers of pollution-causing activities.

Historical Fiction

In historical fiction, there are sources of ecological data to compare to the present. For example, students may develop an awareness of the land as it was seen by early European settlers in North America, by reading *Giants in the Land* (Houghton Mifflin, 1993, 4–6) by Diana Appelbaum, a story of colonial logging of the giant evergreen trees in the early New England forests. Kept intact, the logs were transported to England to be used as masts for ships and to provide supplies for the economic needs of a shipbuilding industry. Additional books about the relationship between animals and humans, the ways humans rely on nature, the effects of humans on the environment, and the ways students have taken social action to make the earth a better place to live are found in the following bibliography.

168 Eckert, Allan W. *Incident at Hawk's Hill.* Illustrated by John Schoenherr. Boston: Little, Brown, 1971.
Environmental Focus: Recognizing relationships between animals and humans

Based on a true event at Hawk's Hill, Manitoba, in 1870, this story tells how six-year-old Ben, a small shy boy, watches, follows, and mimics the movements and sounds of the animals and birds on the Canadian farm home of his parents, the MacDonalds. Following a prairie chicken on the prairie, Ben becomes lost and finds shelter in a badger burrow. The returning badger sees Ben act and talk as she does and she adopts him. The badger brings him eggs and small animals which he eats raw. Ben begins to adopt badger behavior and hunts with her. Two months later, Ben is found by his brother, 16-year-old John. 4–9.

Target Activity: "Being Helped by Animals"

Ask children to consider the ways Ben was helped by the badger. Discuss whether this event could or could not have happened in real life. Ask the students to think of other situations when a human was helped by an animal.

Historical Fiction

The students can be divided into small discussion groups to talk about the situations they have recalled. Finally, each group can select a volunteer to report their responses when they regroup into a total class.

169 Estes, Eleanor (1944). *Rufus M.* Illustrated by Louis Slobodkin. Scarsdale, NY: Harcourt, Brace.
   Environmental Focus: Recognizing ways humans relied on nature during war times
   Though out of print, this story is found in large library collections and is one of the few books that emphasizes ways people relied on Victory Gardens during World War I. Seven-year-old Rufus lives with his mother, his brother Joey, and his sisters Sylvie and Jane in Connecticut during World War I. Rufus helps the war effort by knitting washcloths for soldiers and by raising a crop of vegetables in a Victory Garden. His popcorn partnership with his sister earns enough money for him to become a Victory Boy. The story ends with World War I coming to an end on Armistice Day. 4–6.
   Target Activity: "Relying on Nature's Produce During War Times"
   In this Newbery book about times during World War I, Rufus is a dynamo of energy, a believable character. He pedals his tricycle to the park to ride his favorite horse on the merry-go-round, takes up magic, and practices ventriloquism at school, which earns him time in the class "cloakroom."
   With the students in small groups, the teacher invites them to discuss what they would do to help their nation if the nation were at war as it was during World War I. The students consider such things as: ways to provide clothing and other supplies for the nation's soldiers, ways to provide food for the family, ways they could earn money at their ages, and ways to transport themselves around town without cars and gasoline. Vocabulary unique to the setting should be discussed: cloakroom, Victory Boy, Victory Garden.

170 Holling, Clancy (1951). *Minn of the Mississippi.* New York Houghton.
   Environmental Focus: Understanding an animal's connection to the environment
   As Minn, a snapping turtle, swims downstream, readers learn the history of the Mississippi River Valley through Hollings' thoughtful text and highly detailed illustrations and maps. The "you are there" approach draws in even the most reluctant of readers. 3–5.

Grades 4–8

Target Activity: "How Does Minn Feel about Progress?"

Discuss the idea of "progress" with children. Ask them to consider what progress has done for their lives, e.g., certain inventions such as the washing machine have made our lives easier and allowed us to have more leisure time. Ask children if they think progress is always positive. Introduce some ways that progress has upset the ecological balance in our environment, as when new housing projects encroach upon the natural habitat of creatures like the horned owl, or when pollution from cities threatens our rivers, lakes and oceans. Make two columns on the blackboard, one headed "then" and the other "now." Invite children to consider how Minn's life may have been better and worse in the Mississippi River Valley one hundred years ago as compared with today.

171 Kinsey-Warock, Natalie (1922). *Wilderness Cat.* Illustrated by Mark Graham. Scarsdale, NY: Cobblehill.

Environmental Focus: Surviving in nature

Serena is heartbroken because her family is moving to Canada and her parents say she must leave her beloved cat, Moses, with a neighbor. Even though the family trades with the St. Francis Indians, they do not have enough to eat, so Papa and Serena's brother have to leave to find work. As the family tries to survive the harsh Canadian winter, Moses finds his way to the family, bearing a gift. Children will be attracted to the vivid oil paintings and learn much about the hardships of starting a new life in the 1700s, when families were isolated and survival could not be taken for granted. 4–6.

Target Activity: "Wilderness Journal"

Ask children to keep a journal as it might have been kept by Serena during the harsh Canadian winter, or using the voice of Serena's father or brother as they worked to survive. Invite children to share excerpts from their journals when they are finished.

Write on the board "same" and "different" to head two columns. Ask children to brainstorm what issues would be the same and what would be different in surviving in the Canadian wilderness today as compared with the 1700s.

Optional Activity: "Moses' Journey"

Using a map, have children trace the route that Moses might have taken as he made his way north back to his family in Canada. Ask children to brainstorm some obstacles that the cat might have faced and some fortunate occurrences that might have enabled him to survive the harsh winter. Invite children to write an account of the cat's journey in the manner of *Lassie Come Home.* Encourage children to share their stories with the rest of the class.

Historical Fiction

172 Morrow, Barbara (1990). *Help for Mr. Peale.* Illustrated by the author. New York: Macmillan.

Environmental Focus: Becoming acquainted with supporters of a natural history museum

In the late 1700s, in Philadelphia, Mr. Charles Wilson Peale and his family are moving, and they have artifacts of natural history to contribute to a new museum home, the first American natural history museum in the area. Faced with the problem of how to move such unusual things as exotic plants, large prehistoric bones, and stuffed animals, Peale's son Ruben organizes the children in the neighborhood to form a parade, with its members carrying the items to their new home six blocks away. 4–6

Target Activity: "Valuing Artifacts of Natural History"

Before discussing the story with the students talk about the concept of natural history museums. When discussing the problem of moving items to the new museum, add information from the students' discussion about the characters, setting, problem, and the way it was solved. For those students interested in further information about this subject, suggest that they use other sources to document the establishment of the first American natural history museum in Philadelphia, 1794. Students can report back to the total group to tell what they found when they cross-checked the facts in the book.

173 Turner, Ann (1989). *Grasshopper Summer.* New York: Macmillan.

Environmental Focus: Becoming aware of ways humans have responded to their environment

In this story, the short chapters contain historically accurate details (afterwar attitudes), descriptions, and real characters with personalities. When his father decides to move the family to Kentucky, Sam feels the pain of leaving and going to Dakota Territory. With his family, Sam overcomes obstacles facing them in the Dakota Territory. Making their dugout home and fighting an insect invasion of their crops are just two of the problems they face and resolve. 4–6.

Target Activity: "Friend or Foe?"

Ask children to research what contributions grasshoppers make to ecological systems. What animals use grasshoppers as a food source? Explain to children that some farmers and gardeners consider grasshoppers a nuisance. Ask children to interview one or either of these people to find out why. Have them also find out what actions, if any, are taken to reduce crop damage from grasshoppers in your region. Are pesticides used? Do the actions seem appropriate? Why or why not?

Biographies

Biographies — the accounts of the lives of common and uncommon figures of the past and present — give children an opportunity to appreciate the environmental challenges faced by others. For instance, biography can reflect a naturalist's contributions by showing how a person traveled, met people, and achieved her goal of planting apple trees for pioneers. Indeed, several biographies have depicted the life of a legendary pioneer, John Chapman (1774–1845), who was best known as "Johnny Appleseed" because he devoted his life to planting apple trees. The early pages of M. L. Hunt's *Better Known as Johnny Appleseed* (Lippincott, 1950) focus the reader on Chapman's life in western Pennsylvania, where he worked as an orchardist, and his decision to travel to Ohio country with a bag of apple seeds. He wanted to plant the seeds in the land so the pioneers would have apples when they arrived. He also carried healing herbs and told stories as he traveled west — to western Pennsylvania, Ohio, Indiana and Illinois. The biography's foreword by Hunt makes a comparison for the reader, "there has been growing for more than a century a legend not very different from that of St. Francis of Assisi. It concerns a humble man regarded in his day as an eccentric, but a man who was universally loved in the frontier wilderness country by Indians and white settlers alike." Similarly, *Johnny Appleseed* (Putnam's, 1960) by Gertrude Norman, tells the story of Chapman from his childhood as a boy of seven to his days as an well-liked elderly man in frontier America. *Johnny Appleseed* (Joy Street/Little, Brown, 1990) by Reeve Lindbergh, portrays his life further through rhymes suitable for choral reading.

A partial biography based on the diary of John James Audubon, *On the Frontier with Mr. Audubon* (Coward, McCann, 1977) by Barbara Brenner, tells the story of Joseph Mason, an apprentice painter to John James Audubon, a man who was obsessed with his paintings. In the 1800s, Mason journeyed with Audubon on an expedition down the Mississippi River to collect and make drawings of birds. To develop Mason's point of view, Brenner has recreated Audubon's diary entries as a journal that Mason would have kept.

Several additional biographies about the points of view of ecologists,

Biographies

naturalists, conservationists, caring friends of the earth, and advocates for the environment and living creatures, are found in the following section.

174 Anker, Debby, and John de Graf (1993). *David Brower: Friend of the Earth.* Illustrated by Antonio Castro. New York: 21st Century Books.

Environmental Focus: Becoming aware of a conservationist's interest in preserving the earth

This thoughtful biography reviews the life of the conservationist and photographer, David Brower, who was the first executive director of the Sierra Club and the founder of Friends of the Earth. Brower was nominated twice for the Nobel Peace Prize. 4–7.

Target Activity: "Role Playing an Environmental Advocate"

Distribute role playing cards that describe vignettes from the life of David Brower to children, ask them to research the information they need in Anker and de Graf's book, and then have them act out the parts. Events to consider in creating the cards:

1. two or three citizens of the times talking to each other about the most successful and least successful parts of Brower's career;

2. Brower telling how he served as a conservationist before he became a nominee for the Nobel Prize;

3. two newspaper editors telling some of the things that Brower stood for in the field of conservation; and

4. two or three members of a conservationist group telling why Brower was recognized for his work and the reasons why they think he was nominated for the Nobel Prize two times.

Optional Activity: "Create a Nature Trail"

A nature trail is a wonderful way to use your school yard, but because it requires physical effort and knowledge of flora, you may want to enlist the help of some volunteers, such as natural science students at a nearby college. Any wooded area can house your trail; just clear a path of undergrowth, rocks, or roots — anything on which the children could trip. Fallen limbs can be used as trail markers. The natural science experts can label the flora along the trail so that children can learn to identify them.

175 Bryant, Jennifer (1993). *Margaret Murie: A Wilderness Life.* Illustrated by Antonio Castro. New York: 21st Century Books.

Environmental Focus: Becoming aware of a conservationist's point of view

Grades 4–8

This fascinating book portrays the conservationist Murie's loyalty to her family, and the difficult life she and her biologist husband had living outside the mainland United States. They studied the ecology of Alaska's frontier and were advocates of wilderness preservation. 4–6.

Target Activity: "Design a Community"

Ask the students to close their eyes and try to visualize the community in which they live — if they live in a city, or if there is a city nearby, ask them to visualize how the city looks. Next ask them to try to visualize what that area might have looked like before the city or community was built in that spot. What plants were common to the area? What animals? Was there water in the area? What was the topography of the land?

Ask for a group of volunteers to find out what the land, vegetation, and wildlife were like in their area before the community was built. Ask the volunteers to report back to the rest of the students in one week (sources could include province, state, city, or country historical societies, libraries, etc.). The volunteers should report both verbally and visually. For example, they should list the descriptive characteristics of the plant life in the area and identify the kinds of animals, and the food and water sources upon which that wildlife depended. Have the volunteers describe their findings thoroughly enough that the rest of the students can get a clear picture of what the area was like before it was developed.

Next, ask all of the students to divide into cooperative groups of four or five and have them develop a new community in this natural predeveloped area. Ask them to develop a community in which Margaret Murie would be happy to live; one in which people live and work with the least negative impact on the existing plant life, air quality, water, soil and wildlife, yet meet the needs of the people.

176 Conley, Andrea (1992). *Window on the Deep: The Adventures of Underwater Explorer Sylvia Earle.* Illustrated by James Carraway. New York: Watts.

Environmental Focus: Becoming aware of ways underwater explorers protect the environment of the seas

This is the story of Earle, a marine biologist, diver and underwater explorer who loves science. This love has taken her as deep as 3,000 feet in a solo dive. Discusses the recent technology that has assisted Earle and other divers as they explore the steep undersea valleys in the bed of the sea. Includes diagrams, maps, photographs, bibliography, glossary, and index. 4–7.

Target Activity: "What Do You Want to Know?"

Biographies

Engage interested students in locating other resources and finding other facts about this marine biologist. What more can be discovered about her hard work diving and exploring the deep waters and steep underwater valleys, her use of diving technology, and her love for science?

Optional Activity: "Foods from Aquatic Environments"

Ask students to make a list of all the food items they would expect to find in a supermarket that came directly from an aquatic environment. They may need help with what constitutes an aquatic environment: everything from ocean to pond, from swamp to river is appropriate.

Obtain permission from the manager of a local supermarket to bring your class to the store to find out how many food items actually come from watery habitats. Have the students divide into three-person teams and design a form to record information related to this activity.

177 Faber, Doris, and Harold Faber (1991). *Nature and the Environment.* New York: Scribner's.

Environmental Focus: Becoming aware of people who make a difference in our environment

This biographical book is part of the Great Lives series and gives a historical view over the past 200 years about selected people who have been environmental enthusiasts and "made a difference" in ecology. Some names such as Audubon, Darwin, Roosevelt, and Thoreau will be familiar ones to American students, while other names, especially the people outside the United States, will be unfamiliar to many. 5 up.

Target Activity: "Taking the Role of Someone Who Made a Difference"

With partners, engage the students in taking the role of one or more of the following people who made a difference for our environment. Ask them to find out more about each person (or situation) and incorporate some of what they found into writing suggestions for others for playing the role. Ask students to distribute cards and select roles. Ask them to change roles and repeat the activity. Suggest to students that the role cards can include these ideas:

1. Take the role of a person who became the first forester in America.

2. Take the role of a person who was the first one to believe that Americans should have parks to enjoy in urban areas.

3. Take the role of a person who believes that Americans should have a Conservation Service.

4. Take the role of a person who went on the first motorized scientific expedition.

Grades 4–8

5. Take the role of a person who lives for two years by a pond in a small cabin you built yourself. You make friends with the birds, beasts, and fish, and become close to nature and at peace with yourself.

6. Take the role of a person who believes that there is a pattern in nature that can change or maintain continuity in living things. You call this pattern "evolution" and many people do not believe in your theory.

7. Take the role of a person fascinated with birds. You draw illustrations of the beautiful creatures for others to see and appreciate.

178 Fleischman, Paul (1992). *Townsend's Warbler.* New York: Harper.

Environmental Focus: Becoming aware of the discoveries of naturalists

This is a dual biography about the experiences and discoveries of John Townsend, physician, taxidermist, and naturalist, and Thomas Nuttall, naturalist, that focuses on their journey west in 1834. Through their experiences, a reader learns about the species of birds that migrate in a range from Central America to Mexico to American's Northwest. Fortunately, Townsend obtained two specimens of the bird which Nuttall named "Townsend's Warbler." Maps on endpages included. 4–6.

Target Activity: "What Does It Take to Be a Naturalist?"

Ask the students to discuss the various characteristics of a naturalist in a small group with a discussion facilitator. They may use information found in this biography about Townsend and Nuttall. What other characteristics do they think is needed by a naturalist? Ask students to find out all they can about how a person might be guided toward being a naturalist. In addition to reading more biographies, they might write to naturalists at a nearby college, university or state agency, and ask, "What does the career goal, 'becoming a naturalist' mean to you?"

179 Force, E. (1990). *John Muir.* New York: Silver Burdett.

Environmental Focus: Becoming aware of a naturalist's interest in preserving the environment

This book portrays the life of John Muir (1838–1914), a revered California naturalist, who had an interest in preserving the wilderness. The interesting text discusses his travels and his research about glaciers. 7 up.

Target Activity: "The Muir Scene"

Discuss the writing of a script for a brief skit using the character of John Muir. Working in groups, the students talk about the task. Write a dramatic script for a "scene" between John Muir and one of the other explorers of the glaciers. In the script, encourage the students to include important information about the people and events. Invite children to perform the skit for other classes or for a parents' night presentation.

180 Goodall, Jane (1988). *My Life with the Chimpanzees*. New York: Minstrel Books.

Environmental Focus: Becoming aware of the contributions of a biologist

Jane Goodall grew up in the environment of a well-to-do English family and could have lived an easy, privileged life. Instead, her dream was to spend her life in another environment — in Africa studying animals. At 26, she first entered the forests of Africa to study chimpanzees in the wild. On her expedition, she braved the dangers of the jungle and survived encounters with wild animals in the African bush. She has documented her adventures with chimpanzees. The discoveries she made about them and their relationships to us have gained her worldwide recognition.

Jane Goodall's autobiography gives an amazing account of a person pursuing a dream and not giving up. She attributes the positive happenings in her life to "good fortune," but also she says that "the other kinds of good things are those you make happen through your own efforts. ...I refused to give up, even when it seemed very difficult."

Target Activity: "A Letter to Jane"

Ask children to share what they would choose to be if they could be anything they wanted to be. Discuss the improbability of Jane Goodall's dream. Ask the students why they think she succeeded in realizing her dream against impossible odds. Ask students if they can think of other famous people who have contributed something to our knowledge of living creatures and the environment, e.g., George Washington Carver, etc. Tell children they are going to write a letter to Jane Goodall, or another famous person who was mentioned. Have them include the following in the letter:

1. Why they admire the person.
2. How the world is a better place because the person succeeded.
3. Their own ambitions in life.
4. Questions they would like to ask the famous person about his or her contributions to living creatures and the environment.

Grades 4–8

181 Lowe, Steve (1990). *Walden*. Illustrated by Robert Sakuda. New York: Greenwillow.

Environmental Focus: Becoming aware of the relationships of a naturalist with nature

Henry David Thoreau lived for over two years on the edge of a pond in a small cabin he built himself. He made friends with the birds, beasts, and fish, and though his life was bare in human comforts, he was close to nature and at peace with himself. This book contains carefully selected excerpts of Thoreau's *Walden*, chosen for the older picture book reader. The linoleum cuts provided by the artist, Robert Sakuda, bring to the text the stark natural beauty that it deserves. Notes about Thoreau's life are included in the introduction. 4–6.

Target Activity: "Living Alone with Nature"

Have students imagine it is summer vacation and they will be spending one week alone in the woods living in a rustic cabin by a pond. Remind them that they will have no electricity or running water; this will severely curtail their normal routine. Have them create a diary of how they spend the week, encouraging them to think how they might try to take walks, reflect by the pond, and make friends with the creatures they meet. Invite those who wish to share excerpts from their diary. Do they now think they would like to try this experience? Why or why not?

Optional Activity: "Making a Good Environmental Situation out of a Bad One"

Discuss with the students how they might use what they know to turn "bad" environmental situations into good ones. Read to students a book reflecting problems in the environment. Taking the problems one at a time, brainstorm some ways they could have made these bad situations into good ones. Divide students into groups of three or four and allow them to pick events from the book for sketches that show "before and after" scenes related to an environmental problem.

182 Swift, H. (1962). *From the Eagle's Wing: A Biography of John Muir*. Illustrated by L. Ward. New York: Morrow.

Environmental Focus: Becoming aware of a naturalist's interest in preserving the environment

Born in Scotland, Muir is one of the first people to realize that forests should be protected by our government. It is largely through Muir's influence that Yosemite and Sequoia National Parks are established. He is honored in 1908 for his ideas on conservation when a redwood forest in the Coast Range of California is named Muir Woods. Biography. 6 up.

Biographies

Target Activity: "If I Were to be a Naturalist ..."
After reading this book with students, explain that being a naturalist — John Muir's career — may not appeal to everyone. Then ask them to take a few minutes and think about the reasons they would or would not like to be a naturalist, and tell others their thoughts with, "If I Were to be a Naturalist, I ..." or "If I Were to be (pursuing another environmental career) I ..."

Ask the children to think for a few minutes about the most exciting and interesting career that they could possibly imagine. Then ask them to also "dream big" and write a paragraph that begins, "If I could be anything I wanted to be, I'd ..." and tell about what career they would choose and why. Write the children's choices on the board and then show them how to categorize the career choices in groups. Especially note the careers that relate to the environment, as Muir's did.

Careers That Relate to the Environment	Other Careers
1.	1.
2.	2.

183 Talmadge, K. S. (1993). *John Muir: At Home in the Wild.* Illustrated by Antonio Castro. New York: 21st Century Books.
Environmental Focus: Becoming aware of a naturalist's interest in preserving the environment

The book recounts Muir's difficult childhood in Scotland and Wisconsin, summarizes his inventions and achievements (including his crossing of a glacier that now bears the Muir name in his honor), describes his protection of wilderness areas, and ends with his death in 1914. Included is a map of the John Muir Trail. 3–5.

Target Activity: "Expedition Plan"
Ask the students to suppose they were members of Muir's glacier exploration team and, knowing what they know about the problems and dangers of the expeditions, how would they plan an expedition from beginning to end? If desired, use the following Expedition Plan form:

Problem Situation	Problem Solution
1.	1.
2.	2.
3.	3.

Optional Activity: "Tribute to Someone Who Helped the Environment"

Grades 4–8

Invite the students to think about the things they have seen someone do to protect the environment, and to pay tribute to that person who has shown that he or she cares about the environment. What events can they recall when they recognized someone who made this contribution? Discuss any situations related to caring for the environment that the students have experienced that now cause them to say: 1) I should have... 2) If only I had not ... Distribute sheets of paper for Reflection Pages for student writing of these thoughts and others.

Information

Interested in fostering environmental awareness, several authors of informational books develop their points of view as themes. In this way, the authors can incorporate their beliefs related to ecology. For older students, the themes can become data springboards to launch them into debate and individual inquiry, two activities that are appropriately suited to nonfiction material. Students can begin debates by selecting one side of an ecological issue that is presented by an author and researching additional sources to develop their own points of view.

Portrayals of people's tender feelings toward creatures can also be found in science material about biological life. *Monarchs* (Harcourt, 1992, 4–7) by Kathryn Lasky, shows students the life and migration cycle of the monarch butterfly. The author introduces the caring people who demonstrate how to hatch a chrysalis and discuss ways they protect the monarch's wintering sites in California and Mexico.

Additional books about creatures that are endangered, the value of beautiful wild rivers, the effects of pollution on the habitat of living creatures, and the ways students have taken social action to make the earth a better place to live are found in the following section.

184 Cassidy, John (1994). *Earthsearch*. San Francisco: Klutz.
   Environmental Focus: Recognizing the effects of humans on the planet
   Billed as a "children's geography museum in a book," this volume inspires children to learn. The reader can tell this is no ordinary textbook before it is even opened: the front cover is made from a recycled Russian Coke can! Every single page pulses with high energy graphics and fascinating facts. The book puts the concept of ecology into a broader context and shows how the actions of human beings have a profound effect on the planet. Trash, hunger, population growth, the global economy — all such complex problems are explained using simplified examples and related activities. 2–6
   Target Activity: "Human Cause; Environmental Effect"

Grades 4–8

Have children help you make a list on the blackboard of all the environmental concerns mentioned in this book. Ask each child to select one of the concerns and, using large poster board and magic markers, create a poster that shows humans engaging in an activity that caused the problem. Invite each child to present his or her poster to the class with a brief discussion about what the person in the poster is doing and what that person could do differently to be kinder to the earth. Display the posters in a prominent place in the school under the heading "Human Cause; Environmental Effect"

185 Cone, Molly. (1992). *Come Back, Salmon.* New York: Watts.

Environmental Focus: Becoming acquainted with salmon and the effect the environment has on their behavior

Cone's book is a chaptered portrayal of a project taken on by students from the Jackson Elementary School in Everett, Washington, that consisted of cleaning up the polluted Pigeon Creek near their school. To do this, the students raised "fry," baby Coho salmon, from eggs in a school fish tank and then restocked the creek. Observing the salmon in the water, the students discovered that the fry stayed there for a while as they grew but then followed their natural instinct to journey down-creek to the ocean. Realizing that the salmon would grow to maturity in the ocean and were "supposed to return" to the creek to spawn (and die), the students were concerned that the salmon would not return to the creek because none had returned to Pigeon Creek for several years. However, two and a half years later, some of the salmon did return to spawn, an event widely noted in the news media in Washington and the nation. 4–8.

Target Activity: "Descriptive Words; Descriptive Action about the Salmon"

With students, review the text and identify the descriptive language. Reread the descriptive words, write them on the board, and invite the students to say them aloud as a choral reading. Repeat the activity by asking the students to suggest their ideas for oral interpretation of the words (reading fast, slow; reading high, low; reading excitedly, softly and calmly, line-a-student, duets, unison, etc.). Begin with this description of the salmon: "As it moves through the water, its silver back glistens. Its body is fat and its muscles taut. It is at the peak of its strength."

With students, identify social actions that could be taken related to a polluted animal habitat in their area. Write the students' suggestions on the board and invite the students to consider what steps should be taken to accomplish the action as well as what obstacles might impede any or all of the actions.

Information

Optional Activity: "Life Cycle of the Salmon"

Ask the students to write a report on the life history of one of the species of salmon (e.g., chinook, king, chum or dog, pink or humpback, Coho or silver, sockeye or red, Atlantic). Have them create a mural showing the life cycle of their chosen salmon. Then have children research and illustrate the life cycle of a local fish. Discuss how the life cycle of a salmon is similar to and different from the life cycle of the local fish.

186 Downer, Ann (1992). *Spring Pool: A Guide to the Ecology of Temporary Ponds.* New York: Watts.

Environmental Focus: Becoming acquainted with temporary ponds

Downer's text shows student-naturalists what to look for in ponds and how to draw field maps, and gives examples of guidelines for protecting animals and their habitats near temporary ponds. The ponds are formed by melting snow and rain that attract plant and animal life. Humans have protected the ponds and built toad and salamander tunnels to help the animals stay off roads dangerous to their lives. The appendix includes physical descriptions, diet, life cycle and photographs of specific plants and animals. Full-color photographs included. 4–6.

Target Activity: "Designing a Temporary Pond as a Project"

For students interested further in this project, read aloud *The Living Pond* (Watts, 1990) by Nigel Hester, and discuss his directions for designing a pond as a project. Refer to Downer's book to review some of the possible effects of environmental hazards on a designed pond and talk about what effect acid rain or building a development on the land might have on the pond. Either outside in the school yard, in the neighborhood or inside on a sand table, engage students in designing a temporary pond as a project.

Optional Activity: "Studying a Pond"

Have students set up an action team and locate a pond in your community. Have them list the number of wildlife creatures they observe using the pond. Through interviews with local authorities as well as through their own observation, ask them to determine the overall quality of the wetlands with which the pond is connected. Ask them to report this information back to the whole class.

187 The Earthworks Group (1991). *Kid Heroes of the Environment.* Berkeley, CA: Earthworks Press, Inc.

Environmental Focus: Taking environmental action; becoming acquainted with ways students have made the earth a better place to live

Grades 4–8

The Earthworks handbook is about students in grades two to twelve who have done something to make the earth a better place to live for all living creatures. For each project, there is a summary, a review of what the children did, the results that were gained, and sources for getting more information in case a student wants to get involved in that particular project. There are more than twenty-five exciting stories about the things that "real" students are doing to protect the planet, with details about how other children can do them, too. The book is an inspiring, easy-to-read guide that contains, among others, the following vignettes:

- A repertory theatre group from Los Angeles performs plays about saving the earth;
- In West Covina, California, two girls started a neighborhood recycling center in their front yard;
- Students from Santa Cruz visited schools all over the country to talk about the environment.

This book also includes a resource section at the end with addresses for children's ecological groups and groups that recognize the projects that students are doing. 4–8.

Target Activity: "Kid Hero Search"

After reading *Kid Heroes of the Environment* with the students, invite your class to go on a search for local heroes of the environment. Through the school or local paper or through posters put up around the school and community, advertise that you are searching for any young person (6–18) who is doing something to help save the Earth, to help other people, or to make your school or community a better place. Select a panel of student judges. Reward worthy entries with a display of their deeds and accompanying photos in a prominent place in the school. Especially commendable entries may be sent to:

Kid Heroes
Earthworks Press
1400 Shattuck Avenue, # 25
Berkeley, CA 94709

188 Grace, Eric S. (1992). *Seals.* Illustrated by Dorothy Siemens. New York: Sierra Club.

Environmental Focus: Becoming acquainted with marine mammals and their environment

Grace's informational book introduces a reader to the specific life cycles of species such as seals, sea lions, and walruses and includes environmental information. The text describes the animals' physiology and has a final summary and chart that portrays the evolution of the marine mammals and their relationship to other animals. 4–6.

Target Activity: "Design a Monument to the Marine Mammals"

After a discussion about the book with the students, integrate art into the discussion and encourage interested students to design a monument that could be built in honor of the marine mammals. Then, ask the students to prepare a speech for someone to give at the dedication of the monument. Ask students to show the draft of the speech to partners for editing, proofreading, and suggestions for changes and improvements. Engage students in rewriting their speeches and then in giving their speeches to partners, to small groups, and then to the whole group.

Optional Activity: "Adopt-a-Marine Animal"

The Oceanic Society, a non-profit organization involved in scientific research, is offering children and adults an opportunity to adopt a dolphin for a tax-deductible donation (about $1.00 per child in a classroom of 35 or more) that will support a research project studying wild spotted dolphins in the waters off the Bahamas. Write for more information to The Oceanic Society at Fort Mascon Center, Building E, San Francisco, CA 94123.

189 Gralla, Preston (1994). *How the Environment Works*. New York: Ziff-Davis.

Environmental Focus: Caring for the Environment

This comprehensive source thoroughly explains basic ecological concepts and explores not only how human activity affects the environment but why we should care. Totally produced on computer, most of the information is presented in full-color graphic spreads that distill the essence of ecology into succinct, easy-to-understand chapters. Though it was written for adults, interested young adults and older children will find the strong graphic presentation and concise writing perfectly suited to their needs. Few ecology books available for youth are this comprehensive *and* comprehensible. 6–8.

Target Activity: "What Can I Do?"

After reading and discussing the book, divide children into several small discussion groups. Ask each group to:

• List five environmental issues.

• List one way that people contribute either directly or indirectly to these problems.

• Identify, describe, and evaluate one way people could lessen their role in contributing to these problems.

Grades 4–8

- As a group come up with several lifestyle changes that will reduce the members' role in contributing to these environmental problems

Have a recorder for each small group share their ideas with the larger group.

190 Hehner, Barbara Embury (1991). *Blue Planet.* Illustrated by Ted Lewis. New York: Gulliver.
Environmental Focus: Appreciating Planet Earth
Based on the IMAX film of the same title, this book takes a captivating look at Earth, its ecosystems, geologic history, and much more. Stills from the film are included as well as photographs from the Smithsonian, outstanding paintings, and other illustrations. The text is lucid, informative, and provocative; it impresses upon readers the fragility of Earth's biosphere while offering, through informational sidebars on a variety of topics, a chance for a healthy Earth in the future. 4–6.

Target Activity: "Appreciating Planet Earth"
Have students go outdoors and pick one spot near a tree, a fence, a brook, a field, or some other spot in nature. Each child should sit by him or herself at least 50 feet from the closest human neighbor. Allow 15 minutes for this activity, or ten for younger children. Ask the students to observe their surroundings in the broadest sense of the word — seeing, touching, smelling, and listening. They should record everything they observe in a notebook.

Then bring the students together for a discussion of what they observed, focusing on the process they went through as well as their list of observations. Did they center on any one area for a long time? Did they continually shift their gaze? How did they attend to hearing and smelling? Practice cupping hands around the ears to simulate animals hearing, blindfolding to cause a compensation toward better hearing, and moistening the undersurface of the nose to increase smelling ability. Repeat the observation activity with these new skills ready to be used. Discuss whether or not observation has been heightened.

191 Holmes, Anita (1993). *I Can Save the Earth: A Kids' Handbook for Keeping Earth Healthy and Green.* Illustrated by David Neuhaus. New York: Julian Messner.
Environmental Focus: Taking environmental action
This thoughtful book departs from any other activity books by presenting descriptions of actual environmental steps taken by children. The book

also contains in-depth chapters that combine suggestions for action with factual information. Holmes provides children with critical information about environmental issues, offers examples of real problem-solving strategies used by others, and lends support to pursuing these issues that concern all humans. Students demonstrating their respect for these proposals by taking actions themselves is the next logical — and hopeful — step. 4–8.

Target Activity: "Environmental Interview"

Initiate a discussion with students about whether or not they think people's attitudes about some topics might change over the years. Fashion in clothing, furnishings, and good fads might serve as examples with which to begin. If not raised by the students, ask them to think of examples of changes in attitudes about the environment, uses of natural resources, lifestyles involving natural resources and the environment, etc. Discuss their suggestions and list the topics they suggest.

Have the students, working in groups of two to four, generate a list of questions relating to environmental issues that can be asked of other students in the school or adults. Some examples might be:
- How do you feel about the environment?
- What are you doing to make the environment a better place?
- Do you recycle? How?
- What general changes, if any, have you seen in society's attitudes toward the environment in recent years?
- What do you see as the greatest challenges to the environment today?
- What recommendations, if any, do you have for solving these problems?

Review the questions generated by the students before they conduct their interviews. The students should be prepared to take notes or tape the interviews. Compile the results of the interviews. Discuss with the students their findings, including changes in attitudes, if any, and what might have contributed to these changes.

192 Jacobs, Francine (1981). *Bermuda Petrel: The Bird That Would Not Die.* Illustrated by Ted Lewis. New York: Lothrop, Lee & Shepard.

Environmental Focus: Recognizing that caring people can change the fate of threatened creatures

When Columbus sailed to America in 1492, there were probably more than a million petrels in Bermuda, the only meeting ground for this species. Soon the petrels were killed in large numbers by European sailors and the hogs and rats that accompanied them. By 1620, the birds were thought to be extinct; one was not seen again until 1906. Then, a dedicated Bermudian named David Wingate started a campaign to save the tiny seabird from extinction. This beautifully written text shows that people who really care about nature and wildlife can actually change the fate of a threatened creature. Adding to the appeal of the book are vivid black-and-white drawings that graphically illustrate the beauty of the sea and the splendor of the ocean-flying petrel. 4–5.

Target Activity: "Acting in the Manner of an Environmental Scientist"
Invite the students to role-play the part of an environmental scientist who has been asked to join with other scientists to write a report on future management of the ocean-flying petrel. Ask the students to work with partners and consider some of the following points in their reports:

1. The future environmental scientist needs to consider the health of the entire ecosystem of the oceans as well as the health of the tiny seabird.

2. The future environmental scientist needs to consider communication with European sailors about the value of the petrel.

3. The future environmental scientist needs to consider the habitat of the petrel to protect its life near the oceans.

Optional Activity: "Collect Ecosystem Data"
Children can count specimens in a small area of the school yard. A one-foot circle of string can be the boundary for counting blades of grass or ants, for example. Larger boundaries can be used to examine the different types of plants in the area. If you have access to a computer, data can be entered into the system and monitored over a period of several months.

193 Johnson, Sylvia A. (1994). *A Beekeeper's Year.* Illustrated by Nick Van Ohlen. New York: Little, Brown.

Environmental Focus: Becoming aware of the relationship between bees and people

This is an informative presentation through the four seasons that shows the beekeeper and the tools and methods used to work around bees. It describes what needs to be done in the spring to introduce a new queen, in the summer to tend to the hives, in the fall to extract honey from the hives, and in the winter to keep the bees warm and safe. Includes full-color photographs, a glossary of related terms, and recipes that include honey.

Target Activity: "A Beekeeper's Daily Journal"
Encourage students to record events from the life of a beekeeper in a daily writing journal. Just as the book recorded the tasks of the beekeeper, the

students may write about the things they imagine they would be doing if they were there working with the beekeeper, the recipes they would prepare using the honey that is harvested, what was learned about the relationship between bees and people, what tools were needed and what methods were used to care for the bees.

194 Kendall, Martha E. (1993). *John James Audubon: Artist of the Wild.* (Gateway Greens Biography.) Brookfield, CT: Millbrook.

Environmental Focus: Appreciating wildlife

John James Audubon's lifelong passion for birds inspired him to try to learn how to draw them in the most realistic way, paving the way for "wildlife art" and leading to a wildlife organization that bears his name. The sensitive text offers an insightful view into the personality and life of Audubon. Moreover, copies of the artist's meticulous paintings encourage students to take an interest in the study of birds and birdwatching. Other books in this series about environmental leaders present the stories of the lives of John Muir, Jane Goodall, and Rachel Carson. 4–6.

Target Activity: "Bird Sketching/Bird Watching"

After having the students pay close attention to the detailed illustrations of birds in Kendall's book, find out which of these birds can be found in your area. An excellent resource for this task is *Birdwatching* (Random House, 1992) by Rob Hume, which provides superb information such as labeled drawings and maps. Then provide the students with colored pencils and white construction paper and ask them to draw their favorite bird from among those that live in their area, using Audubon's paintings and Hume's illustrations to assist them. Have students label their birds and place them on a bulletin board in a prominent place in the classroom. Finally, armed with binoculars (if available) and small notepads, take a walk in a nearby wooded area with students. Ask them to jot down any birds they see that they recognize from the books or from their own sketches.

Optional Activity: "Bird Feeders"

Children can learn to identify birds, discover which birds come to the feeder at which times of the year, and find out which birds eat seeds. Hummingbird feeders draw especially delightful visitors. Birds can also teach different flight strategies — hovering versus gliding, for example — leading to discussions of how inventors often get their ideas from nature.

Grades 4–8

195 Krensky, Stephen (1992). *Four Against the Odds: The Struggle to Save Our Environment.* New York: Scholastic.

Environmental Focus: Becoming aware of heroes and heroines of the environmental movement

This important book for more sophisticated readers is a collection of four chapter-length biographies about well-known environmental leaders. The book includes the stories of Rachel Carson, who raged a battle against pesticide use; John Muir, who established the idea of national parks; Lois Gibbs, who brought national attention to the disaster at Love Canal; and the horrific story of Chico Mendez, who worked to save the rain forests. Even the most reluctant readers will be fascinated by Krensky's insightful presentation of human issues and environmental challenges. 5–8.

Target Activity: "Kid Heroes"

After discussing the four environmentalist leaders in Krensky's book, ask students to brainstorm some ways they can protect the environment. When they have exhausted the possibilities that they are able to offer, introduce the book *Kid Heroes of the Environment* (Earthworks, 1991) by Catherine Dee. This easy-to-read guide details what 25 children did to protect the planet, with suggestions about what your students can do too. Encourage pairs of children to select one idea and present it to the class as an action proposal.

196 Lauber, Patricia (1986). *Volcano: The Eruption and Healing of Mount St. Helens.* New York: Bradbury.

Environmental Focus: Learning from nature about recovery and relationships

Lauber describes the May 18, 1980, volcanic eruption of Mount St. Helens, the most destructive eruption in America's history. Mount St. Helens created a huge science lab where scientists could study the workings of an active volcano and watch the mountain rebuild itself, and where they could study the return of life to land that seemed quite barren. Index included. 4 up.

Target Activity: "What Is Nature's Balancing Act?"

With students, discuss what happened as nature recovered from the eruptions and healed itself with the survivors (fireweed and other plants and animals that lived through the event) and colonizers (chipmunks and other animals and plants that moved in) and links to other life, such as the fish and frogs that survived under the snow and ice-covered lake—and talk about any of nature's interconnections that the students mention.

Ask students to work in small groups to discover further information

Information

about ways that nature recovers from certain phenomena and to discover some of the interconnections that occur in nature.

197 Lavies, Bianca (1992). *Monarch Butterflies: Mysterious Travelers.* New York: Dutton.

Environmental Focus: Becoming acquainted with the wintering grounds of the monarch butterfly

The focus of Lavies' book is on the wintering grounds of the monarch in the Sierra Madre mountains of Mexico and the work of scientists and volunteers who discovered the grounds in 1976. Here, the butterflies are tagged and data about them is gathered to determine facts about their survival. Also, the process of metamorphosis is explained, with photographs showing the monarch's various stages of development. The author's endnotes describe the photographer's adventure while photographing a story on monarchs for the *National Geographic* magazine in 1976. 4–5.

Target Activity: "Tribute to a Monarch Butterfly"

Suggest to students that they write a tribute to a monarch butterfly. Ask them to consider the following ideas for their tribute:

1. Suppose you have been asked to write an obituary for a monarch butterfly to be printed in the class paper.

2. What will you call your tribute? What would you write about this insect?

3. Try to include as much information as you can about the harsh life of the monarch butterfly.

198 Lepthien, Emilie U. (1991). *Wolves.* Chicago: Children's Press.

Environmental Focus: Becoming acquainted with the life cycle of the wolf

Lepthien's book, one in a series called "New True Books," concerns the life cycle of the wolf and its adaptation to climate and differing habitats. Moreover, the text raises the reader's ecological awareness of endangered species by providing information about wolf recovery programs and the Endangered Species Act. At the end of the text is a glossary of "words you should know," that explains adaptation, endangered, etc. The text terminates with a discussion of the controversy surrounding the reintroduction of the gray wolf into the northern Rockies. While this action would restore the natural balance of the elk and bison in the area, hunters and trappers are concerned that the wolves would then kill too much wildlife and cattle. The author then asks the reader, "What do you think?" 4–5.

Grades 4–8

Target Activity: "What Do You Think?"
On the board or overhead, write two columns, one labeled "environmentalists" and the other labeled "hunters and trappers." Under the appropriate heading, have students recall both sets of arguments from the text. Invite interested students to do additional research on the issue and add to the columns. Finally, ask students to consider both arguments and write a persuasive paragraph espousing their view about the pros or cons of reintroducing the gray wolf.

199 Lewis, Barbara (1991). *The Kid's Guide to Social Action: How to Solve the Social Problems You Choose — And Turn Creating Thinking Into Positive Action.* Minneapolis: Free Spirit.
Environmental Focus: Problem-solving about environmental problems
Lewis's guide presents some of the steps to take when you and your students have identified a problem critical to solve in your school or neighborhood. Lists of tips in each section assist in this. Examples of social action are given and reproducible forms are included for brainstorming a problem, drafting a proposal, lobbying, writing a business letter, and sending a news release. Resource section gives information about contact groups, the government, and other sources. 5 up.
Target Activity: "From Your Point of View, Which Environmental Problem Is Most Critical?"
With students, discuss what type of problem they think is critical to solve in the school, neighborhood, community, county, state, country or the world. Brainstorm together and write their ideas on the board. Ask students to give reasons why they think their suggested problem is critical as you review the ideas on the board:

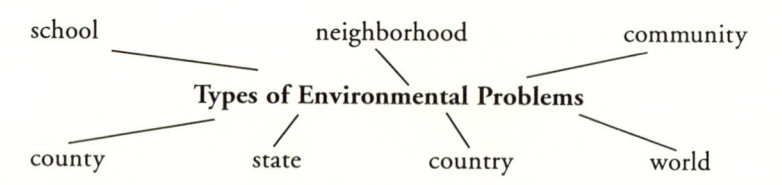

school   neighborhood   community
           Types of Environmental Problems
county   state   country   world

With Lewis's steps from the book, review with the students what needs to be done next and identify the skills that students need to solve the problem. Encourage students to take a special interest, decide to make changes in the environment, and work for the improvement of an environmental problem.

Information

Optional activity: "A Garbage Dump Site Dilemma"
Invite the students to search for a way to take care of the city's garbage and engage them in reading newspapers to do the following:

1. read advertisements in newspapers and the phone book's yellow pages to discover services and products related to taking care of the city's garbage;
2. invite an employee from one of the dump sites to talk to the class;
3. invite an employee from one of the recycling centers to talk to the class;
4. visit a dump site or a recycling center;
5. discuss different solutions to the dilemma;
6. read newspapers and related articles in local and regional magazines to find figures to use in solving the dilemma and calculating the costs of different solutions.

200 Lord, Suzanne (1993). *Garbage: The Trashiest Book You'll Ever Read.* New York: Scholastic.
Environmental Focus: Taking environmental action

The use and abuse of natural resources has a major impact on our planet, as does the creation of a "throwaway" society. Students living near a landfill will find this book especially meaningful to their lives, but others will also appreciate the critical nature of our trash problems. The author uses examples, descriptions, and rather depressing pictures that answer many of the questions that students have about garbage and landfills. 4–6.

Target Activity: "Decreasing Waste"
Label two bags to be used for trash collection:
1. natural resource — vegetation
2. natural resource — mineral

Ask the students to separate all classroom trash into the appropriate bags. Remove regular trash receptacles. At the end of the first week of collection, weigh the containers; record on a chart the two weights and the date. Repeat for several weeks. At the end of four weeks, ask students to multiply the pounds of waste by the number of classrooms in the school. Students will be astounded! Brainstorm ways to decrease the amount of waste generated.

201 Love, Ann, and Jane Drake (1993). *Take Action: An Environmental Book for Kids.* Illustrated by Pat Cupples. New York: Tambourine.
Environmental Focus: Becoming aware of the problems facing animals who try to survive in their habitats; taking environmental action

Grades 4–8

This book by Love and Drake presents the pluses and minuses of happenings in today's ecology on our planet. Including hot environmental issues, a plethora of accessible information, and appropriate opportunities for hands-on simulation, these authors have done a remarkable job inspiring young readers to question current policy and tradition, investigate solutions, and analyze the implications of an overpopulated planet. Verbal portraits of animals enhance a discussion of the problems they have surviving in their habitats. There are visual examples of the text ideas, charts, side panels, and diagrams along with stark black-and-white illustrations. Suggested activities are given. 4–8.

Target Activity: "Take Action!"

With students, review some of the suggested activities in *Take Action* and discuss reasons why that activity would be important or not so important for the students to accomplish. If desired, ask the students to value-rank the activities before a class discussion with 1 as most important, 2 average importance, 3 least important at this time, and 4 not important:

1. write your government representatives to remind them of the Clean Air Act;
2. make sure the beef you order does not come from a rain forest country;
3. carry your personal garbage on your back for a week to make a decision about changing your lifestyle; and
4. raise funds for the World Wildlife Fund. Which activity would the students be interested in doing? Why?

Optional Activity: "Our Crowded Planet"

Introduce the concept of discomfort from overcrowding by asking one student to stand in front of the class. Approach the student slowly, asking him or her to tell you when the closeness is beginning to cause discomfort. Ask the class whether they allow strangers to approach them as closely as they do their friends or family members. How do they feel in the middle of a mass of strangers on a crowded bus or elevator? Discuss what physical reactions they may experience in these kinds of crowded conditions, such as nervousness, avoidance of eye contact, difficulty breathing, and so forth.

Explain that this is just one implication of overpopulation on our planet. Divide students into small groups and have them create a simulation of other implications of overcrowding, such as not enough food, water, or other resources.

Information

202 Lowery, Linda, and Marybeth Lorbiechi (1993). *Earthwise at School.* Illustrated by David Mataya. Minneapolis: Carolrhoda Books.

Environmental Focus: Taking environmental action

This is one in a series of three books written by the same authors and illustrators. The other two books focus on "earthwise" actions at home and at play. Each book provides a combination of excellent photographs and animated drawings to urge students to adopt an environmentally-sound lifestyle. The question and answer formats feature much factual information and culminate in a "call to action" section. The three books in this series inspire our collective responsibility for the preservation of this planet. 4–6.

Target Activity: "What About Trash?"

Have the students predict how much trash and what kinds of materials they throw away in one day. Then collect and save the trash the students in the class generate in one day. Have the students categorize the trash by type of material and then compare this information with their predictions. Ask the students, "Is there anything else we could do with what we throw away?" List their ideas. Most of them will fit into one of the following three categories: reuse, recycle, recover energy. Write these three categories on the board. What trash items might best fit into each category? List them under the proper category heading.

203 McCord, David (1974). *One at a Time.* Illustrated. Boston: Little, Brown.

Environmental Focus: Appreciating the environment through words of a poet

McCord's book contains all of his poems first published in *Far and Few, Take Sky, All Day Long, For Me to Say,* and *Away and Ago.* Elements in the environment are the focus of many of the poems such as "Every Time I Climb a Tree," "Take Sky," "Three Signs of Spring," "Sunfish," and "The Walnut Tree." There is a subject index in the back of the book and a reader can look up the names of creatures such as bugs, fish, frogs, ducks, chickens, to find a related poem. All grades.

Target Activity: "Considering Poems about Nature"

Read aloud McCord's "Earth Song" (p. 43) to the students and discuss his idea for the beginning words: "Let me dry you, says the desert; / Let me wet you, says the sea. / If that's the way they talk, why don't / they talk that way to me?" Demonstrate for the students the thoughts you have about regions you have visited and tell what the regions have "said" to you, e.g., "let me warm you, said the south land, let me cool you said the north." Engage the students in reflecting about the regions in which they have lived or visited and in thinking about what the regions have "said" to them. If desired, engage students in writing brief poems that parallel the rhythm, beat, and word selections of "Earth Song."

Read aloud other poems by McCord about nature, ask students to try to think of a "better" or "exciting" idea for a nature poem and jot down notes about their thoughts as they listen. After the reading aloud, ask students to work with partners and discuss the ideas they had with one another. Let them give one another feedback and have them write the first drafts of their poems. Let students put the poems away — to be tinkered with later (this is working in the manner of McCord) and encourage them to browse through other poetry books about the environment (this is needed tinkering-time that McCord uses, too). Suggest that when the students have edited their poems, and their ideas are in finished form, the students can write their poems on recycled brown paper bag squares and assemble the squares by tying them together at the corners with discarded wire ties, string, or yarn. Display the poems as a large "nature quilt" in the classroom or in the school.

204 McHarry, Jan (1994). *The Great Recycling Adventure.* New York: Turner.

Environmental Focus: Recycling refuse

This compendium of recycling information provides lots of details in a hands-on format. How are paper, metal, plastics, and textiles rejuvenated? Lift the tabs and pull the wheels to find out how garbage is transformed. Illustrations reminiscent of *Where's Waldo* in terms of scale and detail will coax even the most reluctant reader to follow the different processes that sort and convert waste products into raw material for new products. There are only six double-page spreads but they contain a bookload of information. 1–6.

Target Activity: "Thinking about Recycling"

Ask children to close their eyes and reflect for a few moments on their daily lives. Ask them to follow themselves through a typical day, paying special attention to mealtimes. What beverages, foods, dry goods, and other materials do they use that require packaging? Ask students to now open their eyes and help you make a list of all the materials they use in a given day. For each type of material, e.g., paper, metal, glass, plastic, etc., make a separate category on the blackboard. Ask children what happens to each of these items when they finish with them. Do they recycle? Finally, review the processes

Information

explained in the book for each of these materials as they are transformed into new products. Have children make a consumer pamphlet outlining this information.

205 Maynard, Thane (1993). *Saving Endangered Species: A Field Guide to Some of the Earth's Rarest Animals.* New York: Watts.
Environmental Focus: Recognizing various endangered animals
In alphabetical order, the author presents all of the mammals from the white-cheeked gibbon to the red panda Others are shown in close-up photographs, and facts about the mammal's characteristics, habitat and current endangerment are presented for each one. This is a well-organized ecological book that is ideal for helping young readers develop proficiency with informational books. It provides students with many interesting facts about the threats to survival of certain animals and the history of those threats. Illustrations include full-page photographs of the featured animals as well as location maps and summary tables. Additionally, the book provides readers with a list for further reading and with addresses of many environmental awareness groups. 4–8
Target Activity: "Friends of Wildlife"
Organize a group of interested children into a "Friends of Wildlife" club that could meet during recess, free time, or after school. At the first meeting, encourage children to commit to protecting endangered mammals, as identified in the field guide, and ask them to create a motto, such as, "When the animals die, we're dead meat." Help them to design a T-shirt with their name and motto. Each club member can draw a small picture and write a slogan to go with it, like "Protect the Animals." These can be printed in squares on the T-shirts. To raise money, help the children sell the T-shirts to children in other classes or hold fundraisers like "Earthday" events, where ecology-oriented arts, crafts, and games are conducted. Money can be donated to organizations that protect mammals, such as:

Save the Manatees
Florida Audubon Society
500 North Maitland Avenue
Maitland, FL 32751

Optional Activity: "Saving Endangered Plant and Animal Life"
Tell students they are going to see and hear a video entitled "Wyland the Artist and 'Save the Whales'" (Garnier-Weythman Prods. [1992], 19700 Fairchild, Irvine, CA 92715) about the need for preserving the whales. This video is narrated by an artist named Wyland, who creates murals of sea

Grades 4–8

creatures, and by a marine biologist, Maris Sidenstecker, who is also the co-founder of "Save the Whales," an environmental group. Ask students to listen to find out how the two environmental activists followed their preservation interests into their present careers.

206 Paladino, Catherine, selector (1993). *Land, Sea & Sky: Poems to Celebrate the Earth.* Illustrated by the selector. Boston: Joy Street/Little Brown.

Environmental Focus: Recognizing that what is seen in nature can be described using words

In Paladino's book, the photographs are matched with nature poems to help students think about the idea that what is seen in nature can be presented in the imagery of an author's poem. Many of the illustrations feature animals. Some show plants and natural habitats. Others show children enjoying nature's environment. 4–6.

Target Activity: "Recognizing Images of Nature in Poems"

With students, read aloud "Until I Saw the Sea," and ask students to imagine a scene after listening to the poem's words. Ask them to share aloud the scenes they imagined and then show Paladino's photograph that is matched to the poem — a snapshot of a happy youngster running in the ocean waves. Select another poem such as "The Wolf," by Georgia Roberts Durston, which tells about a wolf who has a "long, lean face" and turns to took up at the sky; or select another choice from one of the 19 different poems suitable for imagining other scenes from nature.

207 Petrash, Carol (1992). *Earthways: Simple Environmental Activities for Young Children.* Mt. Rainier, MD: Gryphon House.

Environmental Focus: Taking environmental action

This informational book describes a wide range of environmental activities and actions focused specifically on children. The author has amassed a variety of motivational, craft-oriented, nature-inspired projects that are organized by season. Children find this book irresistible. 4–6.

Target Activity: "Environmental Activities Book"

Petrash has provided an outstanding collection of environmental activities that can be considered just a start in an ecologically sound program. Have students break up into cooperative groups of three or four and research an existing activity other than the ones Petrash has presented, or have them create new ones. Have each group write up their activity using the same step-by-step procedure that Petrash uses. Collate final copies of activities into a class environmental awareness book. Highlight one activity a week to consider and carry out as a class.

208 Ransford, Sandy (1992). *Global Warming: A Pop-Up Book of Our Endangered Planet.* Illustrated by Mike Peterkin. New York: Simon & Schuster.

Environmental Focus: Fostering sensitivity to current global issues

This book examines the topics of global warming, rain forest destruction, and ozone depletion. The text, which requires previous sophisticated knowledge of general scientific principles, is mismatched with the gimmick of pop-up illustrations which generally appeals to a younger audience. The illustrations do make a visual impact, however. In one unfortunately jarring picture, the reader can pull a tab which causes a hunter to pop up and club a baby seal. 4–6.

Target Activity: "A Life Map"

After sharing this disturbing book with the students, help them focus on personal solutions that start with themselves. Help them to develop individual "life maps." These include where they want to live when they grow up, whether they want a family, what kind of home they will occupy, transportation they will use, food sources, water uses, the job they aspire to in the future, and the recreational activities in which they will participate. Help them to consider the costs and benefits of each of their choices—both to them personally, to other people in their imagined community, wildlife, other resources, and so forth. Discuss the impact of each child's "life map" on the global issues presented in Ransford's book.

209 Ring, Elizabeth (1993). *Henry David Thoreau: In Step with Nature.* (Gateway Greens Biography.) Brookfield, CT: Millbrook.

Environmental Focus: Fostering an awareness of heroes and heroines of the environmental movement

Henry David Thoreau is believed by many to have been a man ahead of his time—an environmentalist when it was not fashionable to be one. In Thoreau's time, people were focusing on the accurate scientific descriptions

Grades 4–8

of nature, but Thoreau was more interested in a personal coexistence with nature and the implications of such a relationship. Sketches, pictures, and an excerpt from one of his journals make this informative book much more interesting and accessible. 5–8.

Target Activity: "Nature Appreciation Interview"

Discuss with students how keenly Henry David Thoreau was able to observe and appreciate nature. Explain that they are going to do an activity that will help them to become more sensitive to nature.

Divide students into groups of two. Have each pair decide what plant or animal in nature they would like to "interview." You may assist by helping them brainstorm a diverse list of wildlife in your area — from microscopic to huge. The students are then asked to go outside and find their plants or animals, and take turns interviewing them. First, one student asks the questions and the other answers as the plant or animal might; then the students switch roles. Students may take notes, use a tape recorder, or take Polaroid photos.

After "interviewing" the plant or animal, the students can do research to add to the information. Then each pair of students uses its notes as a basis for writing a newspaper article about the plant or animal they "interviewed." Discuss how appreciation for nature occurred as a result of this activity.

210 Ryden, Hope (1992). *Your Cat's Wild Cousins*. Illustrated by the author. New York: Lodestar.

Environmental Focus: Recognizing what a domestic cat has in common with a wild relative

Ryden describes the traits and behavior of the marbled cat, the Canada lynx and 16 other species of a domestic cat's relatives in brief essays and photographs. Emphasizes the endangered state of some of the species and provides the geographical range and scientific names of the animals. 4–6.

Target Activity: "Tales for Change from Damaging to Protecting"

After discussion of the need to protect the environment and ways people have caused damage to animal life in the past, invite students to discuss ways to do the following before writing their thoughts:

Describe how you managed to change from being a "damager" of animals like your cat's wild cousins in your past, and make a reference to it as you write a brief nonfiction biographical sketch about now being "a protector" of the animals in the environment.

Information

211 Sargent, William (1992). *Night Reef: Dusk to Dawn on a Coral Reef.* New York: Watts.

Environmental Focus: Becoming acquainted with animal life at night on a coral reef

Through the use of high speed or slow motion photography and the resulting photographs, Sargent's book introduces things in the undersea world that happen too quickly for people to see. Some examples include scenes of daytime inhabitants who hide at night, creatures stalking their prey, and ways creatures elude their predators. Includes maps showing sites of coral reefs on end pages. 4–7.

Target Activity: "If We Believed the Same Things"

Ask students to consider how life appears difficult when people argue different points of view and don't think exactly alike on issues. Make two columns on the chalkboard, one labeled "advantages" and the other "disadvantages." Solicit some ideas from the students about the positive ramifications of having everyone believe the same; do the same with negative ramifications. Then ask them to decide for themselves which of the two columns provides stronger arguments. Finally, ask them to write a position paper on the advantages and disadvantages of everyone having like points of view. If desired, ask them to use a format similar to the following:

-If We All Believed the Same-

There are many advantages I can think of to living in a world where everyone holds the same beliefs about an issue. These include

_____

There are also many disadvantages to living in such a world. For example

_____

Considering both the advantages and disadvantages of a world where everyone believes the same thoughts about an issue, I feel

_____

212 Simon, Seymour (1987). *Icebergs and Glaciers.* New York: Morrow.

Environmental Focus: Recognizing types of icebergs and glaciers and their effect on our planet.

Simon's book explains how different glacier and iceberg types are formed. It discusses ways glaciers and icebergs move and travel and how they affect life on earth. Photographs and index included. 4 up.

Grades 4–8

Target Activity: "How Can Icebergs and Glaciers Help Life on Earth?"

With students, review Simon's explanation of what might happen in the future and the possibility that icebergs could be used as a source for fresh water in dry land areas. Ask students to meet in pairs and to think of a plan to use icebergs as a source of fresh water. Several steps follow:

1. Engage them in writing their plan and drawing sketches to illustrate their ideas.

2. Back in the whole group, invite the partners to share their ideas with the other students.

3. Then, turn to Simon's explanation and read aloud the excerpt about a plan that calls for mile-long Antarctic icebergs to be towed to countries by powerful tugs and helicopters. Discuss ways to protect them from melting, and the many problems with this idea.

4. Ask students to think further about what some of the problems might be and record them in a list on the board. When the students return to their partners, engage them in discussing a way to solve one or more of the problems on the list that they could share aloud with others. Ask them to make a sketch of their idea before returning to the whole group and presenting their idea(s).

213 Sinclair, Sandra (1992). *Extraordinary Eyes: How Animals See the World.* New York: Dial.

Environmental Focus: Appreciation of nature's creatures

Topical chapters of varied length present the different eye structures of many kinds of animals. The small color photographs serve as informative examples; several views contrast the same item as seen by the human eye and by a different type of animal eye. The pace is brisk and the interesting discussion includes many thought-provoking insights into the whole scheme of evolution. 4–6.

Target Activity: "Seeing Is Believing"

Set up three learning stations in the classroom — one with a kaleidoscope, the second with binoculars or telescope, and the third with a fish-eye mirror (or photos of objects taken with a fish-eye lens on a camera). Have the students visit each station, trying out the different kinds of vision. Ask the students to guess what kinds of animals might have each of these three types of vision, emphasizing that the way an animal sees is a form of adaptation. For example:

• Binoculars — Predatory birds such as eagles, hawks, and owls have acute distance and depth of vision similar to telescopic vision. This allows them to see their prey from great distances.

Information

• Kaleidoscopes — Insects have compound eyes. Each facet of their eye functions like a separate eye and allows them to see to the side, to detect predators.

• Fish-eye Mirror or Photos — Fish have eyes with wide-angle perception. This helps them to see predators, prey, and other food sources.

Finally, discuss with students what each animal's view of the world could be due to its differing vision.

214 Siy, Alexandra (1992). *The Brazilian Rain Forest.* (Circle of Life Series.) New York: Dillon.

Environmental Focus: Fostering awareness of the endangered rain forest

Of all the current books available on the rain forest, this is among the finest in allowing the reader a realistic glimpse into the lushness and beauty that abounds in that environment. From the opening map and full-page fact table to the enjoyable activities in each chapter, the author provides useful information ranging from technical terms to the interdependency of rain forest denizens. She also includes an interesting section on environmental heroes such as Chico Mendez. 4–6.

Target Activity: "More about Tropical Forests"

Books on the tropical forests and their inhabitants are appearing more and more frequently, each with unique perspectives or features. The following such books can be used for extended and continuing inquiries for interested students:

The Great Kapok Tree (Harcourt, Brace Jovanovich, 1990) by Lynn Cherry
Life in the Rainforest (Scholastic, 1990) by Lucy Baker
A Look Around Rain Forests (Willowsip, 1992) by Ed Perez
Rain Forest: A Close-up Look at the Natural World of a Rain Forest (Dorling-Kindersley, 1992) by Barbara Taylor
Stop That Noise! (Crown, 1992) by Paul Geraghty
A Walk in the Rain Forest (Dawn, 1992) by Kristin Joy Pratt
Welcome to the Green House (G. P. Putnam's Sons, 1993) by Jane Yolen

For children who are interested, a free fact sheet about creative fund-raising for saving the rain forests can be obtained by writing to:

Rainforest Action Network
301 Broadway, Suite A
San Francisco, CA 94133

Grades 4–8

215 Stidworthy, John (1992). *Environmentalist.* New York: Watts.

Environmental Focus: Becoming acquainted with the work of an environmentalist

This book guides a reader in making observations, keeping records, constructing items, and conducting tests. It covers such topics as world habitats, the balance of nature, food webs, air and water cycles, soil contents, climate changes, and the greenhouse effect as well as responsible use of the resources in our environment. 4–7.

Target Activity: "The Waste Will Ruin Us"

When a group of students receive blank 3" x 5" index cards, they can work together in pairs to write about what they think are the most pressing environmental problems. They can choose different problems and enter into debates, research additional sources for information, and develop their points of view. Examples of issues from which students can choose sides and present their positions in a debate forum:

Card #1: Smog is the most pressing environmental pollution problem because:

a) smog affects plants, animals and other living things;

b) smog injures leaves, reduces plant yield and quality, and can cause death.

Card #2: The most pressing environmental problem is dumping waste because:

a) trash is thrown everywhere;

b) chlorine, detergent and cleaning liquids are poured into road gutters and sinks.

Card #3: Air pollution is the most pressing environmental problem because:

a) it causes heart and lung diseases;

b) it creates smog which affects children and elderly people;

c) it damages cells in the airways of the respiratory system.

Card #4: The most pressing thing in the environment is solvents because:

a) they are flammable;

b) they are hazardous;

c) they evaporate toxins into the air.

Card #5: Car pollution is the most pressing environmental problem because:

a) it pollutes the air;

b) it is smoke coming from car exhaust pipes that causes people to cough.

Information

216 Stirling, Ian (1992). *Bears.* San Francisco: Sierra Club.
Environmental Focus: Fostering an awareness of bear behavior
Stirling's book has an interesting, informative text; stories from those who have observed bear behavior closely are accompanied by pictures of bears that show close-ups of a grizzly, two exploring bear cubs, a polar bear in the snow, and others. Topics covered include endangerment, the evolution of bears, family tree, their history, and some relationships between mothers and their cubs. Drawings and watercolor maps included. 4–8.
Target Activity: "How to Be Safe Around Wild Animals"
Explore with students some of the reasons why people are interested in becoming environmental activists and learning how to be safe around wild animals. Encourage them to learn more about being safe around wild animals as an environmental activist research project. Help students begin to devise a questionnaire and invite them to give it to others who are willing to help in the research. Discuss the value of giving respondees an envelope with the student's name on it for the return of the questionnaire. Discuss sample questions for the questionnaire such as: 1) What words best describe "being safe around wild animals" to you? 2) What do you think causes a person to be safe around wild animals?

217 Sullivan, George (1992). *Disaster! The Destruction of Our Planet.* New York: Scholastic.
Environmental Focus: Appreciating heroes and heroines of the environmental movement
This book is most straightforward in its message — almost to the point of being depressing. It graphically portrays the impact on our planet of recent environmental disasters such as the Chernobyl meltdown in the former USSR, the dioxin catastrophe in Times Beach, Missouri, and the devastating result of Operation Desert Storm on the Middle East. Although not totally biographical, these stories realistically portray the impact of the disasters on average citizens and show how the heroes and heroines, like Lois Gibbs, emerged. The stories are accompanied by stark black-and-white photographs. 5–8.
Target Activity: "Games for the Environment"
Discuss with students games and activities that may be damaging to the environment, such as putting graffiti on walls and carving initials on trees.
Take students out onto the school grounds to look for evidence of games that have damaged the environment. Ask students what caused the damage and how it might have been prevented.
Ask students to work together in small groups to invent new games that

do not harm the environment, including the plants and animals living there. Interested students could also try to invent games that would improve the environment in some way.

Invite each group to present their games to the other students. Play each of the games. Ask the students to share their feelings about the importance of playing games that do little if any damage to the environment.

218 Taylor-Cork, Barbara (1992). *Weather Forecaster.* New York: Watts.

Environmental Focus: Understanding nature's weather

This book introduces atmosphere, days, seasons, and climates around the world. Explains the concept of air pressure, the Beaufort Scale, cloud formation, water vapor, warm and cold fronts. Discusses hurricanes, tornadoes, lightning, thunder, hail, snow, rain and rainbows. A reader is given directions for making such items as a barometer, anemometer, rain gauge, and sundial. 4–7.

Target Activity: "Be an Environmental Weather Forecaster"

Engage students in related activities such as making observations of the daily weather, keeping records and constructing one of the instruments in the book by following the directions.

219 Temple, Lannis (1993). *Dear World: How Children Around the World Feel About the Environment.* New York: Random House.

Environmental Focus: Taking environmental action

Through drawings and letters from real children, the author portrays children's feelings and attitudes about pollution, pesticides, and other environmental concerns. Included are delightful pictures of the diverse young faces which add to the earnestness of the timely message. The book will certainly inspire young readers to do their part to save the planet. 4–6.

Target Activity: "Compost in the Classroom"

Discuss with children that one way the environment can be improved would be to make compost out of organic waste. Ask the students, "What is organic waste? How much organic waste do you throw away? Could these wastes be used another way?" Make a list on the board of school organic wastes, such as paper, lunch scraps, grass clippings, leaves, etc.

Have the students collect these for a day. Chop them up as small as possible and put them into a plastic bag. Add an equal part of soil to the organic waste and mix it up. Sprinkle it with enough water to make the soil moist but not soggy. Twist the top of the bag and place a rubber band tightly around it. Each day, have children open the bag and stir the contents to provide oxygen for the microbes. Have the students keep a record of the progress of the decay. Total decay should take about one month.

When the material is decayed, you have compost, a good soil conditioner and plant nutrient. Use the compost to plant something, such as a tree or bush to be eventually transplanted to the school grounds.

220 Wolkomir, Joyce Rogers, and Richard Wolkomir (1992). *Junkyard Bandicoots & Other Tales of the World's Endangered Species.* Illustrated by Laurie Davis. New York: Wiley.
Environmental Focus: Becoming aware of endangered species

Each of this book's chapters is devoted to one of several selected endangered species and presents related natural history stories. Chapter titles include, "Lemurs Are Leaping for Their Lives," "The Razorback Sucker Is on the Edge," "If Mussels Had More Muscle, There Might Be More Mussels," and "Will Parrots Keep Talking?" In each chapter, there are facts and statistics about the species and its fight for survival. Pages of "Habitat Close Up" are included. 4-6.

Target Activity: "No Longer Endangered"

Invite interested students to role-play being fish and game commissioners and suggest their criteria for removing a species from their state's endangered species list. For instance, some of the items to consider for criteria for deleting a species could be the following:

1. Removal of a species from the endangered list if the species has died out.

2. Removal of a species from the endangered list if the species is not a separate, distinct species.

3. Removal of a species from the endangered list if the species has been provided a special habitat to accommodate humans' development of an area.

4. Removal of a species from the endangered list because of local economics or politics.

5. Removal of a species from the endangered list only if the species is provided land elsewhere as habitat by land developers or developers can pay the state to help preserve the species and pay for the effects of the construction of the habitat.

6. Other.

Optional Activity: "Reading in the Manner of a Scientist"

Grades 4–8

Introduce students, grade 6 and up, to such reference periodicals as *Discover* (Walt Disney Magazine); *Earth* (Kalmbach) and *Journal of Soil and Water Conservation* (Soil and Water Conservation Society). *Discover* includes scientific puzzles, brief articles on topics such as a way to neutralize the greenhouse effect and a new theory on the dinosaurs' disappearance, and lists of books for further reading. *Earth* depicts the natural processes of the planet with articles about global warming and other topics related to the environment. *Journal of Soil and Water Conservation* supports the proper use of land and water resources with articles about wildlife, forestry and land practices.

Index

References are to entry numbers, not pages.

A

A B Cedar: An Alphabet of Trees (Lyon) 9
ABC of a Summer Pond (Freedman) 116
ABC of Ecology (Milgrom) 116
ABCs of the Ocean (Asimov) 116
About Birds: A Guide for Children (Sill and Sill) 122
Adams, Adrienne 89
Albert, Burton 74
Albert, Richard 1
Alejandro's Gift (Albert) 1
The Algonquin Legends of New England (Leland) 53
Aliens for Dinner (Spinner) 65, 167
Alison's Zinnia (Lobel) 12
All About Pandas (World Wildlife Fund) 129
Allen, Judy 2
Allen, Thomas B. 11, 28, 148
Alphabet Garden (Coats) 12
The Amazing Paper Book (Bougeois) 87
Amazing World of Dinosaurs (Granger and Ford) 91
Amsel, Sherri 75
Anansi Goes Fishing (Kimmel and Stevens) 57
Anker, Debby 174
Annie and the Old One (Miles and Parnall) 31
The Apple and the Moth (Mari and Mari) 105

Apricot ABC (Miles) 116
Archambault, John 108
Aschenbrenner, Gerald 3
Ashabranner, Brent 132
Asimov, Isaac 116
Aunty Pinau's Banyan Tree (Berkey and Lanterman) 5

B

Back in the Beforetime: Tales of the California Indians (Curry and Watts) 159
Bad Luck Tony (Fradin and Scribner) 19
Baker, Lucy 214
Balloons and Other Poems (Chandra) 17
Bang, Molly 76
Bare, Colleen Stanley 77
Baylor, Byrd 4, 78, 79, 133
Bears (Stirling) 216
The Beautiful Christmas Tree (Zolotow and Robbins) 156
A Beekeeper's Year (Johnson and Van Ohlen) 193
Belting, Natalia 47
Berger, Melvin 80
Bergum, Constance R. 93
Berkey, Helen 5
Bermuda Petrel: The Bird That Would Not Die (Jacobs and Lewis) 192
Bierhorst, John 157
Birchall, Brian 6
Birds (Riccluti) 138

171

Index

Birds (Wildsmith) 154
Birdwatching (Hume) 194
Birrer, Cynthia 158
Birrer, William 158
Blow Me a Kiss, Miss Lilly (Carlstrom and Schwartz) 12
Blue Claws (Krudop) 24
Blue Planet (Hehner and Lewis) 190
Blythe, Gary 33
Born to the Land (Ashabranner and Conklin) 132
Bornstein, Ruth Lercher 44
Bougeois, Paulette 87
Bowman, Leslie 142
The Boy Who Lived with the Seals (Martin and Shannon) 60
Brandenburg, Aliki 72
Braren, Loretta Trezzo 83
Brave Irene (Steig) 35
The Brazilian Rain Forest (Siy) 214
Brenner, Barbara 66
Bridge to Terabithia (Paterson) 147
Brown, Dan 136
Brown, Margaret Wise 7
Brown, Mary Barrett 8
Bruchac, Joseph 160
Bryant, Jennifer 175
Bryson, Bernard 47
Bunting, Eve 9
Butterworth, Nick 10
Byars, Betsy 134

C

Caduto, Michael 160
California Blue (Klass) 143
Callaert, Jacques 146
Cameron, Ann 11
Cameron, Elizabeth 81
Canadian Trees A–Z (Mastin) 9
Canyon, Christopher 153
Carle, Eric 82
Carlson, Laurie 83
Carlstrom, Nancy White 12
Carraway, James 73, 176
Carreno, Mada 48
Cassidy, John 184

Castro, Antonio 174, 175, 183
Catalanotto, Peter 67
Caudill, Rebecca 13
Chandra, Deborah 17
Charlot, Jean 119
Chartier, Norman 100
Chen, Ju-Hong 61
Cherry, Lynn 214
Clark, Ann Nolan 14
Cleaver, E. 53
Clements, Andrew 84
Coats, Laura Jane 12
Come a Tide (Lyon and Gammell) 26
Come Back, Salmon (Cone) 185
Cone, Molly 185
Conis, Ted 134
Conklin, Paul 132
Conley, Andrea 176
Conrad, Pam 135
Conservation from A to Z (Green) 116
Cooney, B. 53
Cooney, Gabriel Amadeus 130
Counting Wildflowers (McMillan) 103
A Crocodile Has Me by the Leg: African Poems (Doob) 49
Crow Boy (Yashima) 40
The Crystal Drop (Hughes) 140, 166
The Cuckoo Child (King-Smith and Bowman) 142
Cupples, Pat 201
Curry, Jane Louise 159

D

Dandelion Year (McTrusty) 105
Daughter of Earth: A Roman Myth (McDermott) 53, 158
David Bower: Friend of the Earth (Anker and deGraf) 174
Davie, Helen K. 52
Davis, Allen 113
Davis, Deborah 15
Davis, Laurie 220
Dayrell, Elpphinstone 49
Dear World: How Children Around the World Feel About Our Environment (Temple) 219

Index

Dee, Catherine 195
deGraf, John 174
Demeter and Persephone (Proddow and Cooney) 53, 158, 162
DePaola, Tomie 50, 51
The Desert Is Theirs (Baylor) 4, 133
Disaster! The Destruction of Our Planet (Sullivan) 217
Doob, Leonard W. 49
Downer, Ann 186
Drake, Jane 201
Dreamplace (Ella and Catalanotto) 67
Duck, Duck (Miller) 109
Duvoisin, Roger 37

E

Earthsearch (Cassidy) 184
Earthways: Simple Environmental Activities for Young Children (Petrash) 207
Earthwise at School (Lowery and Lorbiechi) 202
The Earthworks Group 187
Eating the Alphabet (Ehlert) 12
Eber, Dorothy 149
Eckert, Allan W. 168
Ecoart: Earth-Friendly Arts & Crafts Experiences for 3–9 Year Olds (Carlson and Braren) 83
Ehlert, Lois 12, 16, 85
Endicott, James 108
Environmentalist (Stidworthy) 214
Esbensen, Barbara 52
Estes, Eleanor 169
Ets, Marie Hall 17, 18
Evans, Katherine 24
The Ever-Living Tree: The Life and Times of a Coast Redwood (Vieira) 153
Everybody Needs a Rock (Baylor and Parnall) 79
Extraordinary Eyes: How Animals See the World (Sinclair) 213

F

Faber, Doris 177
Faber, Harold 177
The Fascinating World of Snakes (Julivert) 106
Fink, Joanne 3
Fire Bug Connection: An Ecological Mystery (George and Brown) 136
The Flawed Glass (Strachan) 152
Fleischman, Paul 178
Flock of Birds (Zolotow and Bornstein) 44
Follett, Dwight W. 86
Forberg, A. 53
Force, E. 179
Ford, Pamela Baldwin 91
Four Against the Odds: The Stuggle to Save Our Environment (Krensky) 195
Fradin, Dennis B. 19
Frank, Phil 20
Freedman, Judi 116
Freeman, Don 21
From the Eagle's Wing: A Biography of John Muir (Swift and Ward) 182

G

Gackenbach, Dick 87
Gammell, Stephen 26
Garbage: The Trashiest Book You'll Ever Read (Lord) 200
Gargely, Tibor 7
Geisel, Theodore Seuss (Dr. Seuss) 165
George, Jean Craighead 136, 137, 138
Geraghty, Paul 214
Gerstein, Mordecai 53
The Girl Who Loved Wild Horses (Goble) 160
The Giving Tree (Silverstein) 107
Glaser, Linda 88
Glimmerveen, Ulco 89
Global Warming: A Pop-Up Book of Our Endangered Planet (Ransford and Peterkin) 208
Goble, Paul 54, 55, 160

173

Index

Going on a Whale Watch (McMillan) 104
The Golden Bird (Stopl and Postma) 151
Good Hunting, Blue Sky (Parrish and Watts) 68
Good Morning, River! (Peters and Ray) 32
Goodall, Jane 180
Goode, Diane 69
Goudey, Alice 90
Grace, Eric S. 188
Graham, Margaret Bloy 43
Graham, Mark 171
Gralla, Preston 189
Granger, Judith 91
Grasshopper Summer (Turner) 173
The Great Kapok Tree (Cherry) 214
The Great Recycling Adventure (McHarry) 204
The Great White Owl of Sissinghurst (Simmons) 34
Green, Ivan 116
The Greenpatch Gang in the Case of the Contaminated Canine (Frank) 20
The Grey Lady and the Strawberry Snatcher (Bang) 76
Grifalconi, Ann 161
Growing Vegetable Soup (Ehlert) 12
Guralnick, Elissa S. 162

H

Halsey, Megan 63
Hamilton, Virginia 139
Have You Seen the Birds? (Openheim and Reid) 115
Hawk, I'm Your Brother (Baylor and Parnall) 4, 133
Hehner, Barbara Embury 190
Heller, Ruth 92
Help for Mr. Peale (Morrow) 172
Henry David Thoreau: In Step with Nature (Ring) 209
Her Seven Brothers (Goble) 54
Herrera, Velino 14
Hester, Nigel 186
Hidden Animals (Waters and O'Brien) 128

Hide and Seek Fog (Tresselt and Duvoisin) 37
Himmler, Ronald 9
Hirschi, Ron 93
Hodgell, Robert 86
Hodges, Margaret 53, 56, 158
Hodgkinson, Hadley 6
Holling, Clancy 94, 170
Holmes, Anita 191
Hom, Nancy 62
Houses from the Sea (Goudey and Adams) 90
How Summer Came to Canada (Toye and Cleaver) 53
How the Environment Works (Gralla) 189
Hughes, Monica 140, 166
Hume, Rob 194
Humphries, Tudor 2

I

I Can Save the Earth: A Kid's Handbook for Keeping the Earth Healthy and Green (Holmes and Neuhaus) 191
Icebergs and Glaciers (Simon) 212
If I Built a Village (Mizymura) 111
Iktomi and the Boulder: A Plains Indian Story (Goble) 55
In My Mother's House (Clark and Herrera) 14
Incident at Hawk's Hill (Eckert and Schoenherr) 168
The Indian Heart of Carrie Hodges (Peake and Allen) 148
Isadora, Rachel 70
Island Rescue (Martin) 29

J

Jack, the Seal and the Sea (Aschenbrenner and Fink) 3
Jacobs, Francine 192
Jam, Teddy 22
John James Audubon: Artist of the Wild (Kendall) 194

Index

John Muir (Force) 179
John Muir: At Home in the Wild (Talmadge and Castro) 183
Johnny Appleseed (Norman and Carraway) 73
Johnson, Lonni Sue 84
Johnson, Steve 30
Johnson, Sylvia A. 193
Julie of the Wolves (George) 137
Julivert, Maria Angel 106
June Mountain Secret (Kidd) 141
Junkyard Bandicoots & Other Tales of the World's Endangered Species (Wolkomir, Wolkomir, and Davis) 220
Just Me (Ets) 17

K

Kahee the Cautious Kiwi (Birchall and Hodgkinson) 6
Kastner, Jill 58, 163
Kate Shelley and the Midnight Express (Wetterer and Ritz) 71
Keepers of the Animals: Native American Stories and Environmental Activities for Children (Caduto and Bruchac) 160
Keepers of the Earth: Native American Stories and Environmental Activities for Children (Caduto and Bruchac) 160
Kells, Valeris A. 118
Kendall, Martha E. 194
Kennaway, Adrienne 95
Kid Heroes of the Environment (The Earthworks Group) 187, 195
Kidd, Nina 141
The Kid's Guide to Social Action: How to Solve the Social Problems You Choose and Turn Creative Thinking into Positive Action (Lewis) 193
Kimmel, Eric A. 57
King, Patricia 23
King-Smith, Dick 142
Kinsey-Warock, Natalie 171
Klass, David 143
Koch, Michelle 96
Krensky, Stephen 195
Krudop, Walter Lyon 24

Krupinski, Loretta 88
Kuhn, Dwight 97

L

Labrasca, Judy 15
Land, Sea & Sky: Poems to Celebrate the Earth (Paladino) 206
Lanterman, Raymond 5
Lasky, Katheryn 25
Lauber, Patricia 196
Lavies, Bianca 98, 197
Leedy, Loreen 99
The Legend of the Bluebonnet (DePaola) 50
The Legend of the Indian Paintbrush (DePaola) 51
Leland, C. G. 53
Lent, Blair 49, 56
Lepthien, Emilie U. 198
Let's Go to a Paper Mill (Perkins) 87
Levitt, Paul M. 162
Lewis, Barbara 193
Lewis, Ted 190, 192
Life in the Rainforest (Baker) 214
Lily Pad Pond (Lavies) 98
Listen to the Rain (Martin and Archambault) 108
Little Creek Big River (Follett and Hodgell) 86
Little Elephant's Walk (Kennaway) 95
The Little Island (MacDonald and Weisgard) 102
The Living Pond (Hester) 186
Lloyd, Megan 80
Lobel, Anita 12, 100
Lobel, Arnold 100
Locker, Thomas 101, 144
Loggerhead Turtle: Survivor from the Sea (Scott) 99
A Look Around the Rainforest (Perez) 214
Look Out for Sea Turtles! (Berger and Lloyd) 80
The Lorax (Geisel) 165
Lorbiechi, Marybeth 202
Lord, Suzanne 200
Lottridge, Celia Barker 58

175

Index

Love, Ann 201
Lowe, Steve 181
Lowery, Linda 202
Luenn, Nancy 59, 163
Lyon, George Ella 9, 26, 67

M

M. C. Higgins, the Great (Hamilton) 139
Mabel the Whale (King and Evans) 23
McClosky, Robert 110
McConnell, Keith A. 27, 116
McCord, David 18, 203
McCrephy's Field (Myers and Myers) 112
McDermott, G. 53, 158
MacDonald, Golden 102
McHarry, Jan 204
McMillan, Bruce 103, 104
McTrusty, Ron 105
Maestro, Betsy 106
Maestro, Biulio 106
Major, Beverly 28
Manor, Wendell 46
Manson, Christopher 107
Margaret Murie: A Wilderness Life (Bryant and Castro) 175
Mari, Enzo 105
Mari, Iela 105
Markle, Sandra 145
Martin, Bill, Jr. 108
Martin, Charles E. 29
Martin, Rafe 60
Mastin, Colleayn O. 9
Mayer, Anne 30
Maynard, Thane 205
Might Tree (Gackenbach) 87
Miles, Miska 31, 116
Milgrom, Harry 116
Milkweed Days (Yolen and Cooney) 130
Miller, Edna 109
Mills, Patricia 110
Minn of the Mississippi (Holling) 170
Mizymura, Kazue 111
Monarch Butterflies: Mysterious Travelers (Lavies) 197
Monroe, Jean Guard 164
The Moon Jumpers (Udry and Sendak) 38

Morrow, Barbara 172
The Most Beautiful Place in the World (Cameron and Allen) 11
Mother Earth's Counting Book (Clements and Johnson) 84
My Daniel (Conrad) 135
My First Book of Nature: How Living Things Grow (Kuhn) 97
My Island Grandmother (Lasky and Schwartz) 25
My Life with the Chimpanzees (Goodall) 180
Myers, Christopher A. 112
Myers, Lynne Born 112

N

The Name of the Tree (Lottridge and Wallace) 58
Nature and the Environment (Faber and Faber) 177
Ness, Evaline 13
Neuhaus, David 191
Never Grab a Deer by the Ear (Bare) 77
Night Reef: Dusk to Dawn on a Coral Reef (Sargent) 211
Nine-in-One Grr! Grr! (Xiong, Hom, and Spagnoli) 62
No Dodos: A Counting Book of Endangered Species (Wallwork) 127
Norman, Gertrude 73
Norris, Luanne 113
Nunes, Susan 61

O

An Oak Tree Dies and a Journey Begins (Norris, Smith, and Davis) 113
O'Brien, Teresa 128
The Ocean Alphabet Book (Pallotta) 116
An Ocean World (Sis) 124
O'Donnell, Elizabeth Lee 114
On the Far Side of the Mountain (George) 138
One at a Time (McCord) 18, 42, 203

Index

One Blowy Night (Butterworth) 10
Openheim, Joanne 115
Our Earth, a Multitude of Creatures (Roop, Roop, and Kells) 118
Outside and Inside Trees (Markle) 145
Over Back (Major and Allen) 28

P

Paddle-to-the-Sea (Holling) 94
Page, Valerie King 146
Paladino, Catherine 206
Pallotta, Jerry 116
Parker, Nancy Winslow 117
Parnall, Peter 4, 31, 78, 79, 133
Parrish, Peggy 68
Paterson, Katherine 147
Peake, Katy 148
Pelicans (Wildsmith) 155
Perez, Ed 214
Perkins, Lynn 87
Persephone and the Springtime (Hodges) 53, 158
Persephone, Bringer of Spring (Tomaino and Forberg) 53, 158
Peter Pitseolak's Escape from Death (Pitseolak and Eber) 149
Peterkin, Mike 208
Peters, Lisa Westberg 32
Petrash, Carol 207
Pi Gal (Page and Callaert) 146
Pinkney, Jerry 123
Pitseolak, Peter 149
The Plant Sitter (Zion and Graham) 43
Planting a Rainbow (Ehlert) 12, 85
Play with Me (Ets) 18
Pocketful of Cricket (Caudill and Ness) 13
Postma, Lidia 151
Pratt, Kristin Joy 214
Proddow, P. 53, 158

R

Rain Drop Splash (Tresselt and Weisgard) 125

Rain Forest: A Close-up Look at the Natural World of a Rain Forest (Taylor) 214
Ransford, Sandy 208
Ray, Deborah Kogan 32
The Reason for a Flower (Heller) 92
Red Leaf, Yellow Leaf (Ehlert) 16
Reed-Jones, Carol 64
Regan, Laura 131
Reid, Barbara 113
Riccluti, Edward R. 138
Ring, Elizabeth 209
Ring of Earth: A Child's Book of Seasons (Yolen and Wallner) 105
Risk n' Roses (Slepian) 150
Ritz, Karen 71
Robbins, Ruth 156
Roche, Carolynn 162
Roop, Connie 118
Roop, Peter 118
The Rose in My Garden (Lobel and Lobel) 100
Rufus M. (Estes and Slobodkin) 169
Ryden, Hope 210
Rylant, Cynthia 69

S

Sailing with the Wind (Locker) 144
Sakuda, Robert 181
The Salamander Room (Mayer and Johnson) 30
Sargent, William 211
Saving Endangered Species: A Field Guide (Maynard) 205
Say It! (Zolotow and Stevenson) 45
Say Something (Stoltz) 36
Schindler, S. D. 34
Schlein, Miriam 119
Schmidt, Karen Lee 114
Schoenherr, John 168
Schwartz, Amy 12, 25
Schweninger, Ann 120
Scott, Jack Denton 99
Scribner, Joanne 19
The Seal and the Slick (Freeman) 21
The SeAlphabet Encyclopedia Coloring Book (McConnell) 116

177

Index

Seals (Grace and Siemens) 188
The Seashore Book (Zolotow and Manor) 46
Seashore Story (Yashima) 41
The Secret of the Seal (Davis and Labrasca) 15
Sendak, Maurice 38
Seya's Song (Hirschi and Bergum) 93
Shannon, David 60
Shelby, Anne 121
Sheldon, Dyan 33
Shub, Elizabeth 70
Siemens, Dorothy 188
Sill, Cathryn 122
Sill, John 122
Silverstein, Shel 3, 107
Simmons, Dawn Langley 34
Simon, Seymour 212
Simont, Marc 126
Sinclair, Sandra 213
Singer, Marilyn 123
Sis, Peter 124
Siy, Alexandra 214
Slepian, Jan 150
Slobodkin, Louis 169
Smith, Howard L., Jr. 113
Someday a Tree (Bunting and Himler) 9
Song for the Ancient Forest (Luenn and Kastner) 59, 163
Song to Demeter (Birrer and Birrer) 158
Spagnoli, Cathy 62
Spinner, Stephanie 65, 167
Spowart, Robin 85
Spring Pool: A Guide to the Ecology of Temporary Ponds (Downer) 186
Springtime (Schweninger) 120
Stanley Bagshaw and the Twenty-two Ton Whale (Wilson) 39
The Star Maiden (Esbensen and Davie) 52
Steig, William 35
Stevens, Janet 57
Stevenson, James 45
Stewart, Edgar 116, 164
Stidworthy, John 215
Stillman, Susan 74
Stirling, Ian 216

The Stolen Appaloosa and Other Indian Stories (Levitt, Guralnick, and Roche) 162
Stoltz, Mary 36
Stop That Noise! (Geraghty) 214
Stopl, Hans 151
The Story of May (Gerstein) 53
Strachan, Ian 152
Sullivan, George 217
Summer of the Swans (Byars and Conis) 134
The Sun Is a Golden Earring (Belting and Bryson) 47
Suzan, Geraldo 48
Swift, H. 182

T

Take a Look at Snakes (Maestro and Maestro) 110
Take Action: An Environmental Book for Kids (Love, Drake, and Cupples) 201
A Tale of Antarctica (Glimmerveen) 89
Talmadge, K. S. 183
Taylor, Barbara 214
Taylor-Cork, Barbara 218
Temple, Lannis 219
They Dance in the Sky (Monroe, Williamson, and Stewart) 164
3 Pandas Counting (Halsey) 63
Tiddalick the Frog (Nunes and Chen) 61
Time of Wonder (McCloskey) 27
Tomaino, S. F. 53, 158
Townsend's Warbler (Fleischman) 178
Toye, W. 53
Tracks in the Sand (Leedy) 99
The Travels of the Youth Matsua (Carreno and Suzan) 48
The Tree in the Ancient Forest (Reed-Jones) 64
The Tree in the Wood (Manson) 107
A Tree Is Nice (Udry and Simont) 126
Tresselt, Alvin 37, 125
Trivas, Irene 121
Turner, Ann 173
Turtle in July (Singer and Pinkney) 123

Index

The Twelve Days of Summer (O'Donnell and Schmidt) 114

U

Udry, Janice May 38, 126
Umbrella (Yashima) 42
The Underwater Alphabet (Pallotta and Stewart) 116
Until the Cows Come Home (Mills) 110

V

Van Ohlen, Nick 193
Vegetable Soup (Modessitt and Spowart) 85
The Very Hungry Caterpillar (Carle) 82
El Viaje del joven Matsua (Carreno and Suzan) 48
Vieira, Linda 153
The Village of Round and Square Houses (Grifalconi) 161
Volcano: The Eruption and Healing of Mount St. Helens (Lauber) 196

W

Wagon Wheels (Brenner) 66
Walden (Lowe and Sakuda) 181
A Walk in the Rain Forest (Pratt) 214
Wallace, Ian 22, 59
Wallner, John 105
Wallwork, Amanda 127
Ward, L. 182
Waters, Sarah 128
Watts, James 68, 159
The Wave (Hodges and Lent) 56
The Way to Start a Day (Baylor and Parnall) 78
Weather Forecaster (Taylor-Cork) 218
A Weed Is a Flower (Brandenburg) 72
Weisgard, Leonard 102, 125
Welcome to the Green House (Yolen and Regan) 131, 214

A Wetland Walk (Amsel) 75
Wetterer, Margaret K. 71
Whale (Allen and Humphries) 2
The Whale's Song (Sheldon and Blythe) 33
What to Do about Pollution ... (Shelby and Trivas) 121
Wheel on the Chimney (Brown and Gargely) 7
When I Was Young in the Mountains (Rylant and Goode) 69
When Will the World Be Mine? (Schlein and Charlot) 119
Where the River Begins (Locker) 101
Where the Sidewalk Ends (Silverstein) 3
The White Stallion (Shub and Isadora) 70
Why the Sun and the Moon Live in the Sky (Elpphinstone and Lent) 49
Wilderness Cat (Kinsey-Warock and Graham) 171
A Wildflower Alphabet (Cameron) 81
Wildsmith, Brian 154, 155
Williamson, Ray A. 164
Wilson, Bob 39
Window on the Deep: The Adventures of Underwater Explorer Sylvia Earle (Conley and Carraway) 176
Windsongs and Rainbows (Albert and Stillman) 74
Wings Along the Waterway (Brown) 8
Wolkomir, Joyce Rogers 220
Wolkomir, Richard 220
Wolves (Lepthien) 198
The Woman Who Fell from the Sky (Bierhorst) 157
Wonderful Worms (Glaser and Krupinski) 88
Working Frog (Parker) 117
World Water Watch (Koch) 96
World Wildlife Fund 129

X

Xiong, Blia 62

Index

Y

Yashima, Taro 40, 41, 42
The Year of Fire (Jam and Wallace) 22
Yolen, Jane 105, 130, 131, 214
Your Cat's Wild Cousins (Ryden) 210

Z

Zen ABC (Zerner and Zerner) 56
Zerner, Amy 56
Zerner, Jessie Spicer 56
Zion, Eugene 43
Zolotow, Charlotte 44, 45, 46, 156

Ref
Z5863
.P6C43
1996

7/29/96

2734025

DISCARDED
MILLSTEIN LIBRARY

FOR REFERENCE
NOT TO BE TAKEN FROM THE ROOM

UNIVERSITY OF PITTSBURGH
AT GREENSBURG
LIBRARY